THE FORTY TWO PRECEPTS OF MAAT, THE PHILOSOPHY OF RIGHTEOUS ACTION AND THE ANCIENT EGYPTIAN WISDOM TEXTS

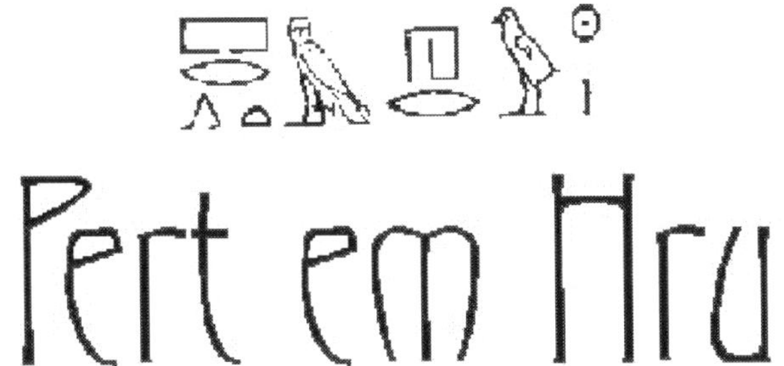

A Course Manual for use with the 1998 Maat Lecture Class Series

by
Dr. Muata Ashby

Sema Institute of Yoga
P.O.Box 570459
Miami, Florida, 33257
(305) 378-5432 Fax: (305) 378-6253

First U.S. edition 1998

The author is available for group lectures and individual counseling. For further information contact the publisher.

Ashby, Reginald Muata

The Forty Two Principles of Maat: The philosophy of Righteous Action
ISBN: 1-884564-48-8

The 42 Precepts of Maat From The Papyrus Written for Ani (18th Dynasty)

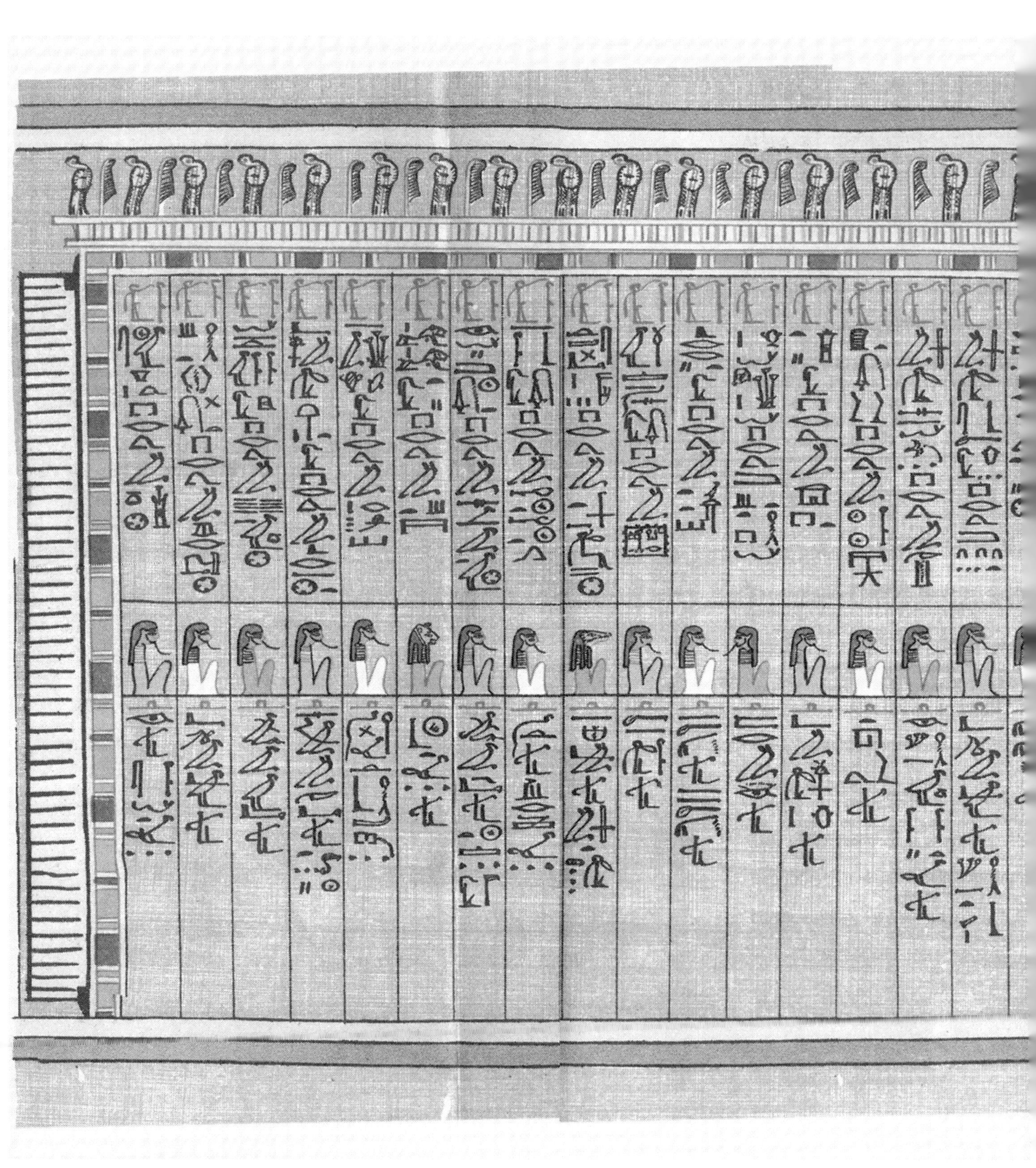

1 2 3 4 5 6 7 8 9 10 11 12 13 14

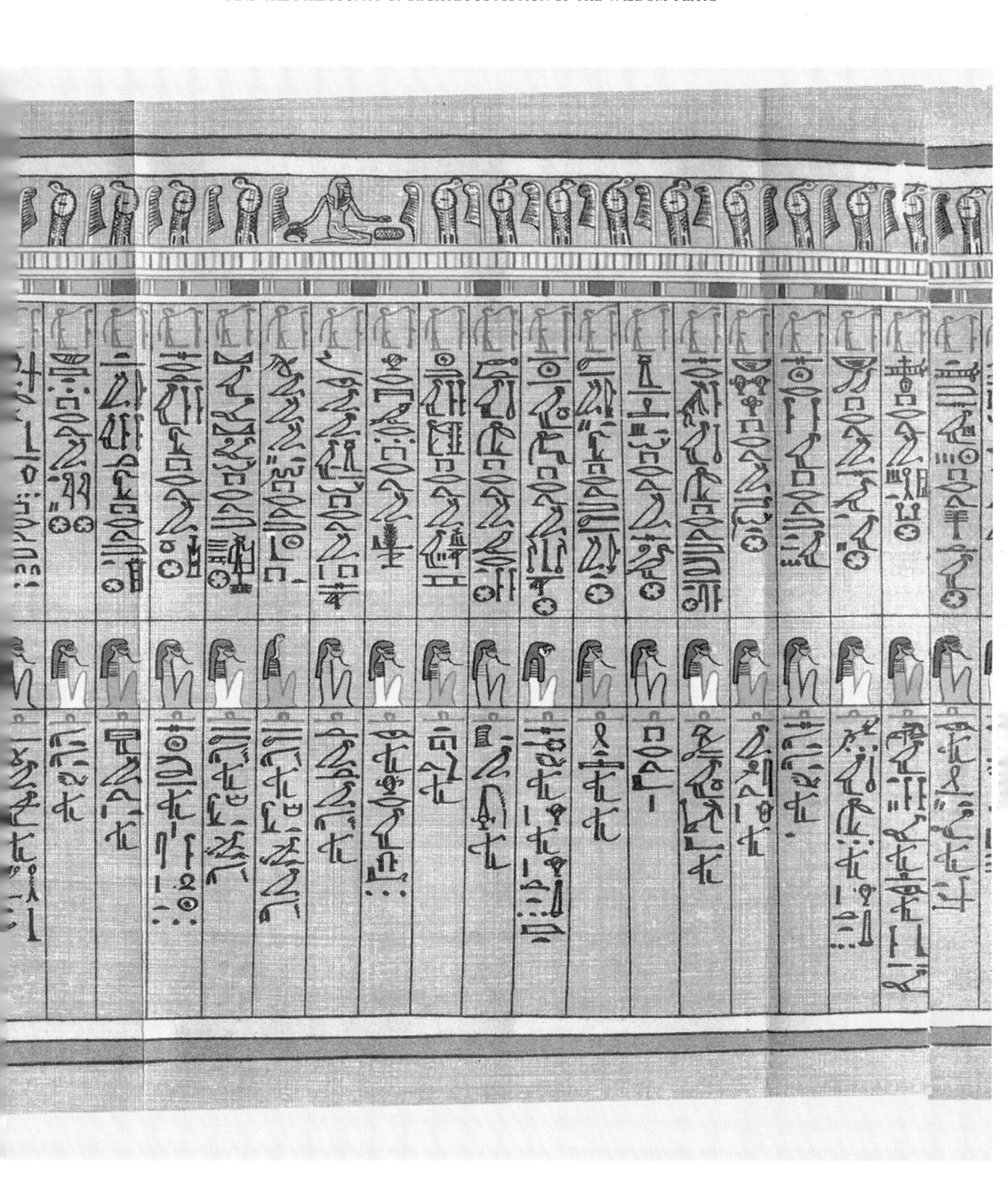

15 16 17 18 19 20 21 22 23 24 25 26 27 28 29 30 31

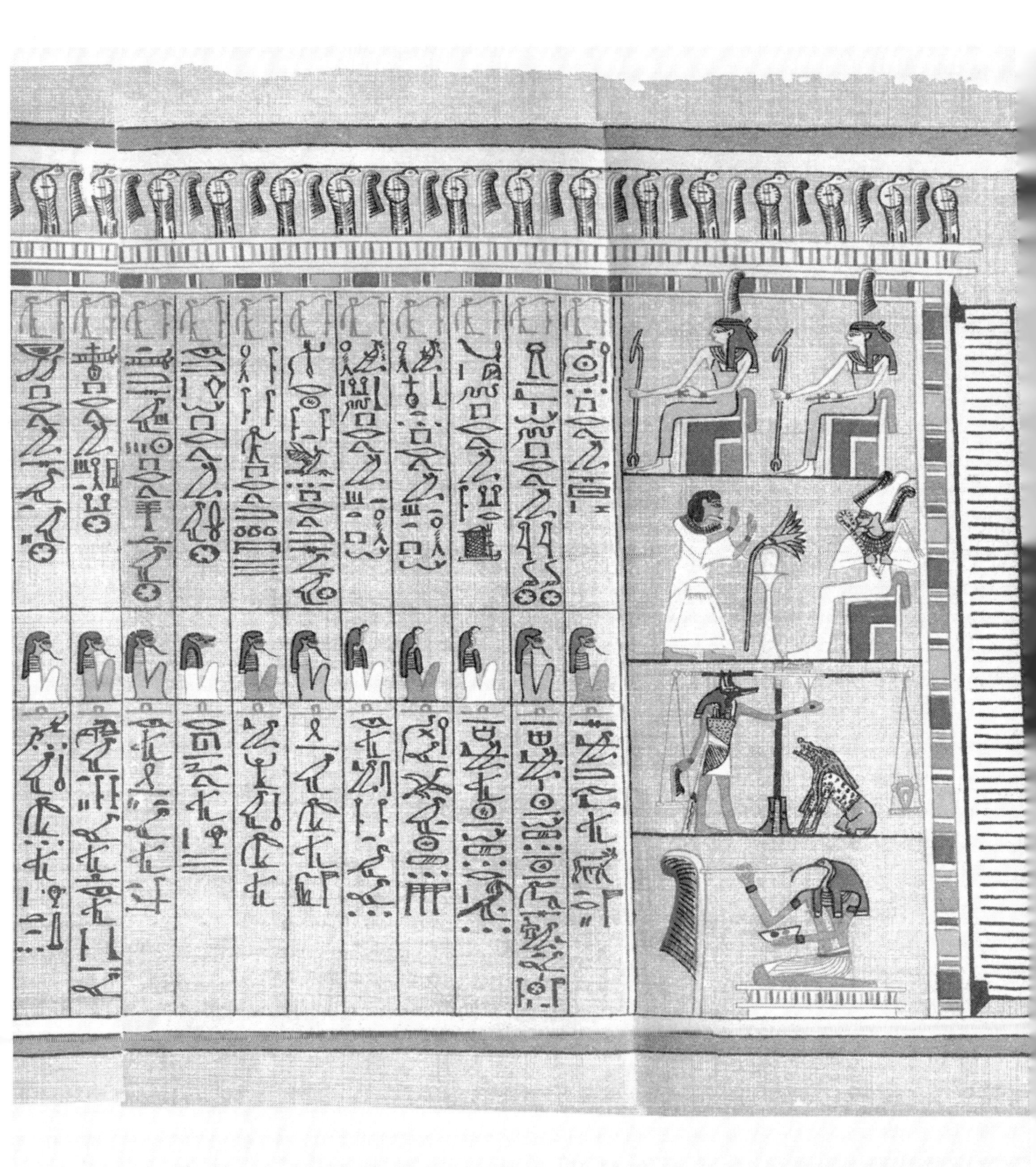

Register 2: Ani propitiates to Asar.
Register 3: Anpu checks the scale.
Register 4: Djehuti records the results.

THE 42 PRECEPTS OF MAAT WRITTEN AS AFFIRMATIONS OF INNOCENCE

(1) “I have not done what is wrong.” Variant: I have not acted with falsehood.
(2) “I have not robbed with violence.”
(3) “I have not done violence (to anyone or anything).” Variant: I have not been rapacious (taking by force; plundering.)
(4) “I have not committed theft.” Variant: I have not coveted.
(5) “I have not murdered man or woman.” Variant: I have not ordered someone else to commit murder.
(6) “I have not defrauded offerings.” Variant: I have not destroyed food supplies or increased or decreased the measures to profit.
(7) “I have not acted deceitfully.” Variant: I have not acted with crookedness.
(8) “I have not robbed the things that belong to God.”
(9) “I have told no lies.”
(10) “I have not snatched away food.”
(11) “I have not uttered evil words.” Variant: I have not allowed myself to become sullen, to sulk or become depressed.
(12) “I have attacked no one.”
(13) “I have not slaughtered the cattle that are set apart for the Gods.” Variant: I have not slaughtered the Sacred bull – (Apis)
(14) “I have not eaten my heart” (overcome with anguish and distraught). Variant: I have not committed perjury.
(15) “I have not laid waste the ploughed lands.”
(16) “I have not been an eavesdropper or pried into matters to make mischief.”
(17) “I have not spoken against anyone.” Variant: I have not babbled, gossiped.
(18) “I have not allowed myself to become angry without cause.”
(19) “I have not committed adultery.” Variant: I have not committed homosexuality.
(20) “I have not committed any sin against my own purity.”
(21) “I have not violated sacred times and seasons.”
(22) “I have not done that which is abominable.”
(23) “I have not uttered fiery words. I have not been a man or woman of anger.”
(24) “I have not stopped my ears listening to the words of right and wrong (Maat).”
(25) “I have not stirred up strife (disturbance).” “I have not caused terror.” “I have not struck fear into any man.”
(26) “I have not caused any one to weep.” Variant: I have not hoodwinked.
(27) “I have not lusted or committed fornication nor have I lain with others of my same sex.” Variant: I have not molested children.
(28) “I have not avenged myself.” Variant: I have not cultivated resentment.
(29) “I have not worked grief, I have not abused anyone.” Variant: I have not cultivated a quarrelsome nature.
(30) “I have not acted insolently or with violence.”
(31) “I have not judged hastily.” Variant: I have not been impatient.
(32) “I have not transgressed or angered God.”
(33) “I have not multiplied my speech overmuch (talk too much).
(34) “I have not done harm or evil.” Variant: I have not thought evil.
(35) “I have not worked treason or curses on the King.”
(36) “I have never befouled the water.” Variant: I have not held back the water from flowing in its season.
(37) “I have not spoken scornfully.” Variant: I have not yelled unnecessarily or raised my voice.
(38) “I have not cursed The God.”
(39) “I have not behaved with arrogance.” Variant: I have not been boastful.[1]
(40) “I have not been overwhelmingly proud or sought for distinctions for myself[2].”
(41) “I have never magnified my condition beyond what was fitting or increased my wealth, except with such things as are (justly) mine own possessions by means of Maat.” Variant: I have not disputed over possessions except when they concern my own rightful possessions. Variant: I have not desired more than what is rightfully mine.
(42) “I have never thought evil (blasphemed) or slighted The God in my native town.”

[1] Bragging, pretentious, arrogant, egoistic.
[2] Selfishness, egoistically.

THE FORTY TWO PRECEPTS OF MAAT, THE PHILOSOPHY OF RIGHTEOUS ACTION AND THEIR FOUNDATION IN THE ANCIENT EGYPTIAN WISDOM TEXTS

SETIY I. (relief at Abydos).

TABLE OF CONTENTS

This Manual was designed for use with the 1998 Maat Lecture Class Series available on Audio Cassette.

To purchase the audio tape set contact:

Sema Institute of Yoga
P.O.Box 570459
Miami, Florida, 33257
(305) 378-5432 Fax: (305) 378-6253

AUDIO LECTURE SERIES ON MAAT PHILOSOPHY

708 Meditation on Maat, chant, breathing, music, Guided visualization
015 Goddess Maat, the Creation and the Philosophy of Karma 1999

Maat Philosophy Series 1998 Lectures Maat, the 42 Laws, the Ancient Egyptian Wisdom Texts

Maat Philosophy Series 1998 Lectures Maat, the 42 Laws, the Ancient Egyptian Wisdom Texts
(Note: Home study Course: This is the next series after the Ausarian Resurrection)
4001 Class 1 - Introduction to Maat Philosophy
4002 Class 2 - Profound issues of Maat and its practice in life
4003 Class 3 - Profound issues and the Cycle of Vice
4004 Class 4 - Introduction to the Principle of Truth
4005 Class 5 - Principle of Truth Part 2
4006 Class 6 - Principle of Truth Part 3
4007 Class 7 - Principle of Truth part 4
4008 Class 8 - Introduction to the Principle of Non-violence
4009 Class 9 - Principle of Non-violence Part 2
4010 Class 10 - Principle of Non-violence Part 3
4011 Class 11 - Principle of Non-violence Part 4
4012 Class 12 – Principle of Non-stealing Part 1
4013 Class 13 – Principle of Non-stealing Part 2
4014 Class 14 – Principle of Non-stealing Part 3
4015 Class 15 – Principle of Selfless Service
4016 Class 16 – Principle of Right Action
4017 Class 17 – Principle of Right Speech Part 1
4018 Class 18 – Principle of Right Speech Part 2
4019 Class 19 – Principle of Right Speech Part 3
4020 Class 20 – Principle of Right Speech Part 4
4021 Class 21 – Principle of Right Worship Part 1
4022 Class 22 – Principle of Right Worship Part 2

4023 Class 23 – Principle of Right Worship Part 3
4024 Class 24 – Principle of Right Worship Part 4
4025 Class 25 – Principle of Right Worship Part 5
4026 Class 26 – Principle of Right Worship Part 6
4027 Class 27 – Principle of Right Thinking Part 1
4028 Class 28 – Principle of Right Thinking Part 2
4029 Class 29 – Principle of Right Thinking Part 3
4030 Class 30 – Principle of Right Thinking Part 4
4031 Class 31 – Principle of Right Thinking Part 5
4032 Class 32 – Principle of Right Thinking Part 6 {The Three States of Mind--Journey of Hathor (Het-Heru)—continues on 4033}- Dr. Karen Dja Ashby
4033 Class 33 – Principle of Right Thinking Part 7 {The Three States of Mind—Journey of Hathor (Het-Heru); Conclusion by Dr. Karen Dja Ashby }
4034 Class 34 – Principle of Right Thinking Part 8
4035 Class 35–Principle of Right Thinking Part 9 (Cleanse the Unconscious mind by Dr. Karen Dja Ashby, cont. on 4036)
4036 Class 36 – Principle of Right Thinking Part 10 (Cleanse Unconscious mind by Dr. Karen Dja Ashby, continued on 4037)
4037 Class 37 – Principle of Right Thinking Part 11 (Cleanse Unconscious mind by Dr. Karen Dja Ashby, conclusion)
4038 Class 38 – Principle of Right Thinking Part 12
4039 Class 39 – Principle of Right Thinking Part 13 (Right Mental Perception)
4040 Class 40 – Principle of Right Thinking Part 14 (Right Mental Perception)
4041 Class 41 – Principle of Right Thinking Part 15 (Right Mental Perception)
4042 Class 42 – Principle of Right Thinking Part 16
4043 Class 43 – Principle of Right Thinking Part 17
4044 Class 44 – Principle of Right Thinking Part 18
4045 Class 45 – Principle of Sex Sublimation Part 1
4046 Class 46 – Principle of Sex Sublimation Part 2
4047 Class 47 – Principle of Sex Sublimation Part 3
4047A Class 47A – Principle of Sex Sublimation Part 3 Q and A
4048 Class 48 – Principle of Sex Sublimation Part 4
4049 Class 49 – Principle of Sex Sublimation Part 5 Workshop How to handle conflicts – Righteous Speaking and Listening
4050 Class 50 – Principle of Sex Sublimation Part 6
4051 Class 51 – Principle of Sex Sublimation Part 7
4051A Class 51A – Principle of Sex Sublimation Part 7 Q and A
4052 Class 52 – Principle of Sex Sublimation Part 8
4053 Class 53 – Principle of Sex Sublimation Part 9
4053A Class 53A – Principle of Sex Sublimation Part 9 Q and A
4054 Class 54 – Principle of Sex Sublimation Part 10
4055 Class 55 – Principle of Sex Sublimation Part 11
4056 Class 56 – Principle of Sex Sublimation Part 12
4057 Class 57 – Maat and the Serpent Power Part 1
4058 Class 58 – Maat and the Serpent Power Part 2

Note: For additional new lectures in this series call Sema Institute www.Egyptianyoga.com

INTRODUCTION

"There are two roads traveled by humankind, those who seek to live MAAT, and those who seek to satisfy their animal passions."

Ancient Egyptian Proverb

The following is a compilation of the 42 laws or precepts of Maat and the corresponding principles which they represent. Maat philosophy was the basis of Ancient Egyptian society and government as well as the heart of Ancient Egyptian myth and spirituality. Maat is at once a goddess, a cosmic force and a living social doctrine, which promotes social harmony and thereby paves the way for spiritual evolution in all levels of society. The Ancient Egyptian Creation myth tells of how God, Ra, created the universe by placing his daughter, Maat, in the place where there was chaos. Maat is the principle of order, harmony, regularity, consistence, peace and truth, which hold the universe together in an orderly fashion. Thus, as a human being that adopts the Maatian lifestyle can come into harmony with the universe (God). Whereas a human being that deviates from Maat will meet with frustration, anxiety, pain and sorrow. In the absence of a social philosophy, which promotes justice, peace and the sublime goals of life, a society cannot function equitably or survive the passage of time. Herein lies the importance of Maat philosophy for the present and future generations.

Other similar social philosophies have developed in other cultures. In India, the philosophy of Dharma, or righteous action, developed. In Christianity the Beatitudes and the new commandments of Jesus serve the same purpose. However, if moral injections are simply memorized but never applied, not understanding their deeper spiritual implications they will not be practiced correctly or at all. Thus the moral character of society declines and strife develops in society. When society places more importance on worldly values and not on spiritual values of life, society declines.

"When opulence and extravagance are a necessity instead of righteousness and truth, society will be governed by greed and injustice."

–Ancient Egyptian Proverb

The injunctions of Maat were statements composed by the Sages of Ancient Egypt and recorded in temple walls and papyrus scrolls, which have survived to this day. They were to be used by spiritual initiates for the purpose of cleansing their personalities and making themselves pure vessels in order to promote spiritual self-discovery. These teachings came to be known as the Book of the Dead. The correct name is *Prt m Hru* or Pert *Em Heru* meaning “Utterances for Coming Into the Light of the Most High (Supreme Self-God)” or “The Wisdom and Practices Which Make one Becoming Spiritually Enlightened.”

THE 42 INJUNCTIONS OF MAAT AS THEY APPEAR IN THE PERT EM HERU

The following is a composite summary of the "negative confessions" from several Ancient Egyptian *Books of Coming Forth by Day*. They are often referred to as "Negative Confessions" since the person uttering them is affirming what moral principles they have not transgressed. In this respect they are similar to the *Yamas* or ethical restraints of India, within the philosophy of Dharma. While all of these books include 42 precepts, some specific precepts varied according to the specific initiate for whom they were prepared and the priests who compiled them. Therefore, I have included more than one precept per line where I felt it was appropriate to show that there were slight variations in the precepts and to more accurately reflect the broader view of the original wisdom imparted by the texts.

(1) "I have not done iniquity." Variant: Acting with falsehood.
(2) "I have not robbed with violence."
(3) "I have not done violence (To anyone or anything)." Variant: Rapacious (Taking by force; plundering.)
(4) "I have not committed theft." Variant: Coveted.
(5) "I have not murdered man or woman." Variant: Or ordered someone else to commit murder.
(6) "I have not defrauded offerings." Variant: or destroyed food supplies or increased or decreased the measures to profit.
(7) "I have not acted deceitfully." Variant: With crookedness.
(8) "I have not robbed the things that belong to God."
(9) "I have told no lies."
(10) "I have not snatched away food."
(11) "I have not uttered evil words." Variant: Or allowed myself to become sullen, to sulk or become depressed.
(12) "I have attacked no one."
(13) "I have not slaughtered the cattle that are set apart for the Gods." Variant: The Sacred bull - Apis)
(14) "I have not eaten my heart" (overcome with anguish and distraught). Variant: Committed perjury.
(15) "I have not laid waste the ploughed lands."
(16) "I have not been an eavesdropper or pried into matters to make mischief." Variant: Spy.
(17) "I have not spoken against anyone." Variant: Babbled, gossiped.
(18) "I have not allowed myself to become angry without cause."
(19) "I have not committed adultery." Variant: And homosexuality.
(20) "I have not committed any sin against my own purity."
(21) "I have not violated sacred times and seasons."
(22) "I have not done that which is abominable."
(23) "I have not uttered fiery words. I have not been a man or woman of anger."
(24) "I have not stopped my ears against the words of right and wrong (Maat)."
(25) "I have not stirred up strife (disturbance)." "I have not caused terror." "I have not struck fear into any man."
(26) "I have not caused any one to weep." Variant: Hoodwinked.
(27) "I have not lusted or committed fornication nor have I lain with others of my same sex." Variant: or sex with a boy.
(28) "I have not avenged myself." Variant: Resentment.
(29) "I have not worked grief, I have not abused anyone." Variant: Quarrelsome nature.
(30) "I have not acted insolently or with violence."
(31) "I have not judged hastily." Variant: or been impatient.
(32) "I have not transgressed or angered God."
(33) "I have not multiplied my speech overmuch." (Talk too much)
(34) "I have not done harm or evil." Variant: Thought evil.
(35) "I have not worked treason or curses on the King."
(36) "I have never befouled the water." Variant: held back the water from flowing in its season.
(37) "I have not spoken scornfully." Variant: Or yelled unnecessarily or raised my voice.
(38) "I have not cursed The God."
(39) "I have not behaved with arrogance." Variant: Boastful.
(40) "I have not been overwhelmingly proud or sought for distinctions for myself (Selfishness)."
(41) "I have never magnified my condition beyond what was fitting or increased my wealth, except with such things as are (justly) mine own possessions by means of Maat." Variant: I have not disputed over possessions except when they concern my own rightful possessions. Variant: I have not desired more than what is rightfully mine.
(42) "I have never thought evil (blasphemed) or slighted The God in my native town."

THE SEMA (YOGA) OF RIGHTEOUS ACTION

"The wise person who acts with MAAT is free of falsehood and disorder."
-Ancient Egyptian Proverb

The teachings of Pert em Heru are related to the Yoga of Righteous Action. The word Yoga originates in the Indian Sanskrit, meaning union of the lower self (mortal personality) with the higher (immortal spiritual Self). Since there is no direct translation for Yoga in the English language and since it has been assimilated into the English language, it will be used as the English translation of the word interchangeably with the Indian Sanskrit term as well as the Ancient Egyptian term. In Ancient Egypt the main word-symbol for Yoga was *Smai* (𓄤). Yoga is the practice of spiritual disciplines, a way of life, which lead to positive spiritual evolution. There are four major aspects of Yoga: The Yoga of Wisdom, The Yoga of Devotion, The Yoga of Meditation and the Yoga of Righteous Action.

The teachings of righteous action originated in the early history of Ancient Egypt with the writings of the Ancient Egyptian Sages, known as the "Wisdom Texts." There were many Sages in Ancient Egypt, however, only a relatively small number of their writings have survived. Nevertheless, these are enough to provide a viable understanding of the Ancient Egyptian wisdom teachings and these writings reveal the source of the Maatian precepts and philosophy contained in the Pert em Heru. Therefore, as we study the precepts of Maat, along with the Wisdom Texts, we will obtain a deeper insight into the profound nature of the precepts.

The Sages of ancient times noticed that action is the inescapable fact of life. Everyone must be engaged in one form of action or another. However, if one's actions are based on ignorance and egoism then they lead to unnecessary entanglements and negative situations in life that ultimately cause pain and sorrow (Negative Karma). The Sages then set out to develop a system of philosophy which will lead a person to act correctly in life and discover the inner reaches of their own higher self. The practice and perfection of action affords a human being the opportunity to purify his or her heart. This leads to a life of peace, harmony with nature and society and ultimately to spiritual enlightenment as well (Positive Karma). The teaching of Karma is embodied in the following Ancient Egyptian teaching from the Instructions of Merikara:

> (14) The Court that judges the wretch,
> You know they are not lenient,
> On the day of judging the miserable,
> In the hour of doing their task.
> It is painful when the accuser has knowledge,
> Do not trust in length of years,
> They view a lifetime in an hour!
> When a man remains over after death,
> His deeds are set beside him as treasure,
> And being yonder lasts forever.
> A fool is who does what they reprove!
> He who reaches them without having done wrong
> Will exist there like a god,
> Free-striding like the lords forever!

Karma is a Sanskrit word which has been assimilated into the English language. The Ancient Egyptian term is Meskhenet. Meskhenet is the accumulated sum total of a person's mental impression which they gathered through their past feelings, desires, and beliefs, based on their previous actions. They are impressions stored in the mind, which impel a person to actions in accordance with the nature of the impressions. There is no equivalent word in the English language for Karma but this Indian word has been assimilated into Western culture. The Ancient Egyptian term for Karma is Meskhenet. Karma is not destiny or fate. It can be changed in accordance with a person's present actions and new understanding. So a person can change a bad situation into a good situation and spiritual ignorance and degradation into spiritual enlightenment by changing the actions in life from unrighteous to righteous, from those based on spiritual ignorance to those based on spiritual wisdom.

The 42 precepts may be classified into six major principles and within these more can be subdivided. The six principles are Truthfulness, Non-violence, Right Action, Right Thinking, Non-stealing and Sex Sublimation. The subdivisions are under Right Action. They are Selfless Service to Humanity, Right Speech and Right Worship of the Divine or Correct Spiritual Practice.

Truth (1), (6), (7), (9), (24)

Non-violence (2), (3), (5), (12), (25), (26), (28), (30), (34)

Non-stealing (4), (8), (10)

Self-Control-Right Action (Living in accordance with the teachings of Maat) (15), (20), (22), (36)

- **Selfless Service**, (29)
- **Right Speech** (11), (17), (23), (33), (35), (37)
- **Right Worship** (13), (21), (32), (38), (42)

Balance of Mind - Reason - Right Thinking (14), (16), (18), (31), (39), (41)

Sex-Sublimation (19), (27)

The number to the left of each precept denotes the order in which it appears in the Papyrus of Ani or Pert em heru of Initiate Ani. Since there are various Pert em Herus which have been discovered and no two have the same exact wording, variants will also be included to elucidate on the expanded meanings accorded to the precepts by different Sages.

Along with each precept the corresponding excerpts from the Wisdom Texts will be included for greater understanding and study. The Wisdom Texts included here have been translated by various Egyptologists and edited by Dr. Muata Ashby.

NOTE: This pamphlet was designed as a manual for use with the 1998 Maat Philosophy Audio Lecture Class Series produced in Miami Florida at the weekly Yoga class conducted by Dr. Ashby at Florida International University. For more detailed studies in the 42 Precepts of Maat and the Wisdom Texts consult the 1998 Maat Philosophy Lecture Series on audio cassette, the book The Ausarian Resurrection, by Dr. Muata Ashby and the book The Ausarian Resurrection by Dr. Muata Ashby, available through the Sema Institute of Yoga (305) 378-6253. INTERNET ADDRESS: http://members.aol.com/Semayoga/index.htm E-MAIL ADDRESS: Semayoga@aol.com

THE JUDGEMENT IN THE PERT EM HERU

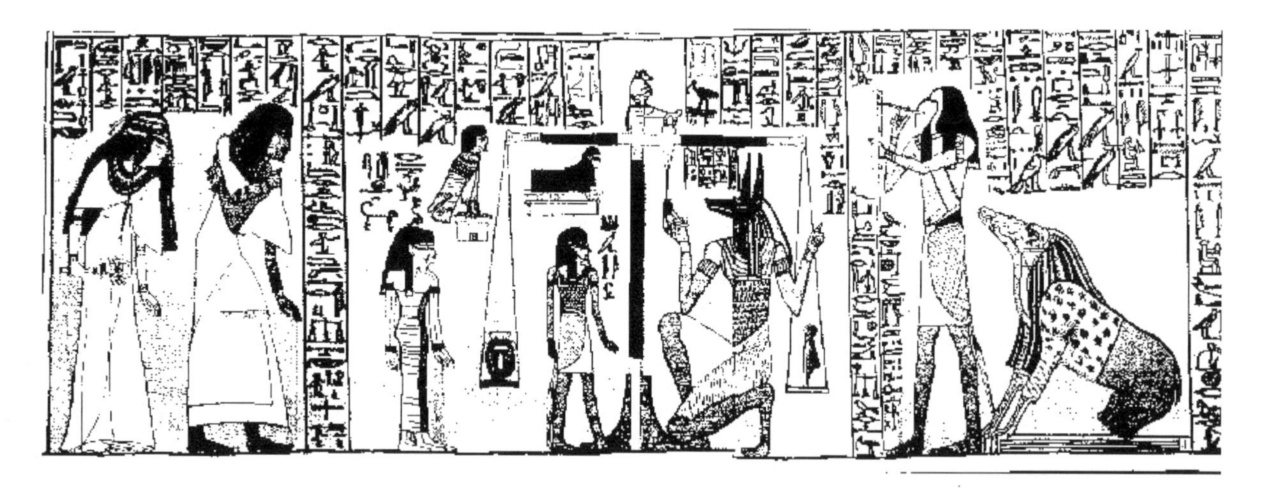

The Maat-Meskhenet (Karmic) Scales and the Hall of Judgment.
The Judgment of the Heart of Ani, from the Funerary papyrus of Ani.

Far left, Ani enters the hall of Judgment. His heart (Conscience) is being weighed by Anubis while the Divine principals Shai, Renenet and Meskhenet look on. Ani's soul and his destiny also look on while Anubis measures Ani's heart against the feather of Maat. At far right Djehuti records the result while the Monster Ammit, the Devourer of the unjust awaits the answer.

The hands of Djehuti (God of wisdom) are "SHAI" which means "destiny" and "RENENET" which means "Fortune and Harvest." The implication is that we reap (harvest) the result of our state of mind (heart). Our state of mind including our subconscious feelings and desires is weighed against cosmic order, Maat. If found to be at peace (Hetep) and therefore in accord with cosmic order (Maat) it will be allowed to join with the cosmos (Asar). Otherwise it will suffer the fate as dictated by it's own contents (mental state of unrest due to lingering desires) which will lead it to Ammit who will devourer the ego-personality and the soul will experience torments from demons until we learn our lessons or become strong enough through wisdom to know ourselves. Demons may be evil cosmic energies it has allowed itself to come in contact with or mental anguish and torments we put ourselves through due to our own ignorance. Self-torment may be regret over some action or inaction while alive or a reluctance to leave because of a lingering desire to experience more earthly pleasure. Therefore, we control our own fate according to our own level of wisdom.

Following the judgment, Asar Ani is taken by the androgynous Heru (note the female-left breast) and introduced to a mummified Asar who holds the Flail, Crook and Was staffs and is enthroned in a shrine surmounted by a Hawk - Heru. Asar wears a crown symbolic of Upper and Lower Egypt and is assisted by Nephthys and Aset. When Ani reaches the shrine, he is justified and glorified as symbolized by the anointing *"grease cone"* on his head (see Anointed One), and kneels with upraised right arm, holding a Sekhem staff in the left. In front of him there is a table of offerings including flowers, fruit and a ***khepesh*** or "foreleg of ox". Above him there are vessels of wine, beer and oils, and at the topmost compartment of the register, there is another offering table with bread, cakes, a wreath and a ***"set"*** or duck.

After being judged and having been found to be worthy (pure of heart), Ani is led by Heru, the Lord of Heaven and Earth (Upper and Lower Egypt), who is Ani's own androgynous soul, to Asar who is Ani's higher self. Ani has acquired the spiritual strength (Sekhem) to become one with Asar and thus will join Asar in Amenta. Ani's offering of the ***"khepesh and set"*** (symbols of male and female principles) represents Ani's relinquishment of his earthly - dualistic consciousness. Thus Ani is offering his ego-consciousness so that he may realize his non-dualistic - all-encompassing cosmic higher self in Asar.

Now Ani's name becomes Asar-Ani. The green Asar, who in this teaching assumes the role of the male aspect of NETER,[3] being supported by Nephthys (death) and Aset (life), is the Supreme deity (Heru) representing *"that which is up there"*. In this aspect, the green Asar' mummified form represents neither existence nor non-existence, neither life nor death but that which lies beyond, the Life Force (green) which vivifies all things. He holds the power of leading one to absolute reality (Shepherd's Crook), the power to emanate Life Force (Was), and the power to separate the mortal human body from the eternal soul just as the winnowing whip or Flail separates the chaff from the seed. Aset and Nephthys (life and death) represent Creation for only in the realm of creation can there be "life" or "death". In the realm of Asar there is only eternal life. From the feet of Asar rises the World Lotus (symbol of creation) with the four sons of Heru (all directions of the compass - meaning all encompassing) standing on it. Asar wears the Atef crown which is composed of the Hadjet crown (Upper Egypt), the Double Plumes crown (Amun) and a small solar disk at the top (Ra) not shown in scene above (see below). Therefore, Asar incorporates the attributes of Heru, Amun and Ra. Thus, to join Asar in Amenta is to join with the attributes of Asar since Amenta is Asar. In this way one's own soul is responsible for its own fate, either to be led by Apep (ignorance)

[3] Other teachings concerning Asar describe an androgynous, omnipotent, hidden, all pervading being who supports all life. In various other texts, the same attributes are ascribed to Aset, Hathor, Heru, Amun, Ra, Ptah, and to other male and female Egyptian Creator divinities. Thus we are led to understand that there is one Supreme Being which is the basis of the Egyptian mysteries, in the same way as the Indian Gods and Goddesses Krishna, Rama, Brahma, Vishnu, Shiva, Saraswati, Kali, Parvati represent male and female aspects of the Supreme Divinity in Hindu mythology.

into the jaws of Ammit (destruction, suffering, reincarnation) or to union with Asar (Hetep-eternal peace). Thus, it is one's own enlightened soul (Heru) who leads one (Ani) to union with one's true self (Asar).

THE SIGNIFICANCE OF THE PRECEPTS OF MAAT AND THE WISDOM BEHIND THE RITUALS OF THE PERT EM HERU

At the time of death or prior to death, the heart (consciousness, Ab) of the human being is weighed against truth, symbolized by the feather of Maat. Here our divine faculties of reason and moral rectitude and our ability to practice the precepts while on earth are judged. Below: The Scales of Maat in the Ancient Egyptian Judgement scene from the *Book of Coming Forth by Day* (Book of the Dead).

In the Hall of Maati, the heart and internal organs of the deceased are judged by the 42 judges (gods and goddesses) who are each in charge of one regulation. All 42 regulations or virtuous guidelines for living make up the basis for the 42 "negative confessions." If one lives righteously, one will be able to say that one has NOT committed any offense. Upon uttering these words, the deceased takes on a new name. For example, instead of Lisa Williams, it is now Asar Lisa Williams.

The objective of life is to become "light of heart." That is to say, one should live a life that is free of stress and which promotes mental peace. When this is possible, the mind relaxes and reveals the divine nature of the soul. If the heart is weighed down by egoism due to a life of worry, lies, frustration, and desire, the heart will be judged as heavier than the feather. Instead of moving forward to join with Asar (God), the deceased, in this case, Asar Lisa Williams, is sent back to the world in the form of an animal if her acts were very sinful or she will undergo reincarnation into a human form to again try to become "light of heart."

If the heart of Asar Lisa Williams is found to be lighter than the feather or of equal weight, it signifies that she has lead a virtuous life and has mastered the *knowledge and wisdom of every god* (all of which are aspects of the one God, meaning she has mastered all 42 precepts) and that she is fit for a new life. Asar Lisa Williams is ready to transcend this world onto the next realm of existence. She is ready to journey back to meet Cosmic Asar, who represents Cosmic Consciousness, her own Higher Self (God).

Asar Lisa Williams, through her own virtuous life, is allowed to take or fashion a new, glorious body, to live in eternity as one with Asar (God). Thus, Asar Lisa Williams, the individual human soul, meets and joins with Asar (God), the Supreme Being. This is the attainment of Enlightenment or the Kingdom of Heaven. This signifies that our own nature is that of universal consciousness. What was separated only by ignorance is now re-united, re-membered. It is only due to ignorance and to distraction in the world of seemingly desirable objects that we think we are individual human beings with bodies, which are mortal. In reality, we are immortal and eternal beings who are one with the universe and each other. Through ignorance, fueled by egoistic desire, we have come to believe that the human existence is all there is. Through the process of living the teachings of Maat or in the case of Christianity, the Commandments and Beatitudes (given by Jesus), the mind can be lightened to such a degree that it allows the soul to behold its true nature unclouded by the passions and desires of the mind.

The objective of all mystical religions and philosophies is to achieve this realization before the time of death. To realize this even before death, it is necessary to live in a virtuous manner, learning the lessons of human existence and uncovering the veil of ignorance, which blinds us from the realization of our essential nature. We must therefore master the knowledge and wisdom of every "god," every precept.

Anubis (god of discernment between reality and illusion) and Djehuti (god of reason and truth) oversee the scales of Maat. They judge the condition of the Heart (Ab) and determine its level of spiritual achievement. This is also symbolized by the Ammit monster, devourer of hearts, who, according to the Ancient Egyptian *Kenna* papyrus, determines those who are the advanced spirits and worthy of salvation (those who have developed their higher consciousness centers: selflessness, peacefulness, universal love, etc.), symbolized by the fourth through seventh rings or levels of consciousness, and those who have not progressed beyond their base animal natures (lower consciousness centers: fear, attachments, egoistic desires, anger, hatred, etc.), symbolized by the lower three rings. The Ammit monsters (demon) symbolically devour the unrighteous.

As in the *Kundalini Chakra* system of India, those who achieve no higher than the level of the third Energy Center or Chakra are considered to be people on the same level of consciousness as animals. They are mostly concerned with satisfying the pleasures and desires of the senses (food, sex, controlling other people) and, therefore, will have to reincarnate in order to further evolve beyond this stage. Upon reincarnating, they will once again have the possibility of confronting situations which will afford them the opportunity to perform correct action and thus, to change. Correct action leads to correct feeling and thinking. Correct feeling and correct thinking lead to a state of consciousness, which is unburdened. This is the goal— to unburden the mind so that consciousness, the soul, may be revealed in its true appearance. When this occurs the soul is discovered to be one with God and not individual and separate. One realizes that the Kingdom of Heaven is within oneself. This is the highest realization of all mysteries, yogas and religious systems.

The Egyptian *Book of Coming Forth By Day* is a text of wisdom about the true nature of reality and also of *Hekau* (chants, words of power, utterances) to assist the initiate in making that reality evident. These chants are in reality wisdom affirmations, which the initiate recites in order to assist him or her in changing the consciousness level of the mind. The hekau themselves may have no special power except in their assistance to the mind to change its perception through repetition with understanding and feeling in order to transform the mind into a still and centered state. Through these affirmations, the initiate is able to change his/her consciousness from body consciousness ("I am a body") to Cosmic Consciousness ("I am God"). Indian Gurus recognize this form of affirmatory (using affirmation in the first person) spiritual discipline as the most intense form of spiritual discipline. However, there must be clear and profound understanding of the teachings before the affirmations can have the intended result. It is also to be found in the Bible and in the Gnostic Gospels as we will see. Compare the preceding statements in the Indian Upanishads and the Christian Bible to the following Ancient Egyptian scriptures (*Metu Neter,* Sacred Speech) taken from the *Egyptian Book of Coming Forth By Day* (c. 10,000-5,000 B.C.E.) and other hieroglyphic texts:

From Indian Yoga wisdom:	From the Bible:	From Ancient Egypt:
"Aham brahma asmi" - I Am the Absolute	On the name of GOD: ***"I Am That I Am."***(The Bible, Exodus 3:14) Jesus speaks of his own origin and identity: ***"I and the Father (GOD) are ONE."*** John 10:30	***Nuk Pu Nuk. ("I Am That I Am.")*** In reference to the relationship between GOD and Mankind: ***Ntef änuk, änuk Ntef. ("He is I and I am He.")***

The 42 declarations of purity have profound implications for the spiritual development of the individual as well as for society. They may be grouped under three basic ethical teachings, *Truth, Non-violence* and *Self-Control.* Under the heading of self-control, three subheadings may be added, *Balance of Mind or Right Thinking Based on Reason, Non-stealing* and *Sex-Sublimation.* The principles of Maat are very similar to the principles of Dharma of India.

The Ancient Egyptians included elaborate scrolls with the mummies of the dead. These were known as the Books of the Dead. The early Coptic Christians also included a Book of the Dead and mummified their dead in keeping with the Ancient Egyptian traditions. The book consisted of sheets of papyrus inscribed with Gnostic Christian texts such as the gospels. Many of these Books of the Dead can be found in the British Museum. One of the surviving books, (Oriental #4919 (2), contains a copy of the Apocryphal letter of King Abgar to Christ and the first words of each of the four Gospels.

MAAT PRINCIPLES OF ETHICAL CONDUCT	Hindu Dharma Principles of Ethical Conduct (From the *Manu Smriti*)
• **Truth** (1), (6), (7), (9), (24) • **Non-violence** (2), (3), (5), (12), (25), (26), (28), (30), (34) • **Non-stealing** (4), (8), (10), (41) • **Right Action- Self-Control (Living in accordance with the teachings of Maat)** (15), (20), (22), (36) • **Right Speech** (11), (17), (23), (33), (35), (37) • **Right Worship** (13), (21), (32), (38), (42) • **Selfless Service** (29) • **Balance of Mind - Reason – Right Thinking** (14), (16), (18), (31), (39) • **Sex-Sublimation** (19), (27)	• Firmness. • Forgiveness, forbearance. • Control of Senses. • Non Stealing. • Purity of body and mind. • Control of mind. • Purity of Intellect. • Knowledge. • Truthfulness. • Absence of anger.

There is one more important factor, which is inherent in the Precepts of Maat that must receive special mention. Generally when people are ignorant of the greater spiritual realities and caught up in the emotionality of human life, they tend to look for something to blame for their miseries. They want to find a cause for the troubles of life and the easiest way to do this is to look around into the world and point to those factors around them, which seem to affect them, be they people, situations or objects. In Chapter 125 of the *Book of Coming Forth By Day,* the use of the word *nuk* ("I") is emphasized with a special connotation. The spiritual aspirant says continually "I have..." He or she does not say "You have allowed me" or "The devil made me do it" or "I wanted to, but I couldn't" etc.

There is a process of responsibility wherein the spiritual aspirant recognizes that he or she has the obligation to act righteously and, in so doing, to purify their own heart. Spiritual practice can succeed only when you assume responsibility for your actions, thoughts, words and feelings. If you constantly blame your adversities on others or on situations, etc., you will be living life according to ignorance and weakness. True spiritual strength comes from leaning upon the Self within for spiritual support and well being, rather than upon external situations, people or objects, even though the help itself may come in the form of external situations, people or objects.

Thus, within the teachings of Maat can be found all of the important injunctions for living a life, which promotes purity, harmony and sanctity. While these may be found in other spiritual traditions from around the world, seldom is the emphasis on non-violence and balance to be found. In Christianity, Jesus emphasized non-violence and in Hinduism and Buddhism, the discipline of *Dharma,* composed of *Yamas and Nyamas,* which are moral (righteous) observances and restraints for spiritual living, emphasizes non-violence. These are the restraints *(Yamas):* Non-violence, Abstinence from falsehood (Truthfulness), Non-stealing, and Abstinence from sex-pleasure. These are the ethical observances *(Nyamas):* Purity, Contentment, Austerity, Study of scriptures (and -repetition of *Mantra-* chanting*),* and Surrender to God.

The Ancient Egyptian, Hindu and Buddhist traditions were the first to recognize the power of non-violence to heal the anger and hatred within the aggressor as well as the victim. When this spiritual force is developed it is more formidable than any kind of physical violence. Therefore, anyone who wishes to promote peace and harmony in the world must begin by purifying every bit of negativity within themselves. This is the only way to promote harmony and peace in others. Conversely, if there is anger within you, you are indeed promoting anger outside of yourself and your efforts will be unsuccessful in the end.

THE WRITINGS OF ANCIENT EGYPT

The earliest utterances of pert em Heru from Ancient Egypt begin with the Pyramid Texts and the Wisdom Texts (5,000 B.C.E.) writen on temple walls and steales. These were copied and expanded in the Coffin Texts (the same writings but now on burial coffins (2,040-1,640 B.C.E.). Then the writings found expression in papyrus as the famous Books of the Dead (1,640-100 B.C.E.). The forty two Precepts of Maat and Chapter 125 in particular, represent a distilation of the vast wisdom of Ancient Egyptian spiritual philosophy which was developed in the remotest periods of antiquity.

Above: Forms of the Ancient Egyptian Goddess Maat.

THE PRECEPTS AND THE VARIANTS

The 42 Precepts of Maat have been rearranged below in accordance with the Maatian Principle that they represent.

TRUTH

(1) "I have not done iniquity (what is wrong)." Variant: Acting with falsehood.
(6) "I have not defrauded offerings." Variant: or destroyed food supplies or increased or decreased the measures to profit.
(9) "I have told no lies."
(7) "I have not acted deceitfully." Variant: With crookedness.
(24) "I have not stopped my ears against the words of right and wrong (Maat)."

NON-VIOLENCE

(2) "I have not robbed with violence."
(3) "I have not done violence (To anyone or anything)." Variant: Rapacious (Taking by force; plundering.)
(5) "I have not murdered man or woman." Variant: Or ordered someone else to commit murder.
(12) "I have attacked no one."
(25) "I have not stirred up strife (disturbance)." "I have not caused terror." "I have not struck fear into any man."
(26) "I have not caused any one to weep." Variant: Hoodwinked.
(28) "I have not avenged myself." Variant: Resentment.
(30) "I have not acted insolently or with violence."
(34) "I have not done harm or evil." Variant: Thought evil.

NON-STEALING

(8) "I have not robbed the things that belong to God." Variant: Or the offerings to the dead.
(10) "I have not snatched away food." Variant: food that belongs to the child.
(41) "I have never magnified my condition beyond what was fitting or increased my wealth, except with such things as are (justly) mine own possessions by means of Maat." Variant: I have not disputed over possessions except when they concern my own rightful possessions. Variant: I have not desired more than what is rightfully mine.

SELF-CONTROL-RIGHT ACTION (LIVING IN ACCORDANCE WITH THE TEACHINGS OF MAAT)

(1) "I have not done iniquity (what is wrong)." Variant: Acting with falsehood.
(15) "I have not laid waste the ploughed lands."
(20) "I have not committed any sin against my own purity."
(22) "I have not done that which is abominable."
(36) "I have never befouled the water." Variant: held back the water from flowing in its season.

SELFLESS SERVICE

(29) "I have not worked grief, I have not abused anyone."

RIGHT SPEECH

(11) "I have not uttered evil words." Variant: Or allowed myself to become sullen, to sulk or become depressed.
(17) "I have not spoken against anyone (slander)." Variant: Babbled, gossiped.
(23) "I have not uttered fiery words. I have not been a man or woman of anger."
(33) "I have not multiplied my speech overmuch." (Talk too much)
(35) "I have not worked treason or curses on the King."
(37) "I have not spoken scornfully." Variant: Or yelled unnecessarily or raised my voice.

RIGHT WORSHIP

(13) "I have not slaughtered the cattle that are set apart for the Gods." Variant: The Sacred bull - Apis)
(21) "I have not violated sacred times and seasons."
(32) "I have not transgressed or angered God."
(38) "I have not cursed The God." Variant: Or ignored The God.
(42) "I have never thought evil (blasphemed) or slighted the God in my native town."

BALANCE OF MIND - REASON - RIGHT THINKING

(14) "I have not eaten my heart" (overcome with anguish and distraught). Variant: Committed perjury.
(16) "I have not been an eavesdropper or pried into matters to make mischief." Variant: Spy.
(18) "I have not allowed myself to become angry without cause." Variant: Not adopted a quarrelsome nature.
(31) "I have not judged hastily." Variant: or been impatient.
(39) "I have not behaved with arrogance." Variant: Boastful.
(40) "I have not been overwhelmingly proud or sought for distinctions for myself (Selfishness)."

SEX-SUBLIMATION

(19) "I have not committed adultery." Variant: And homosexuality.
(27) "I have not lusted or committed fornication." Variant: or sex with a boy.

THE PRECEPTS AND THE WISDOM TEXTS

WHO WERE THE SAGES WHO WROTE THE WISDOM TEXTS?

Ancient Mystical Philosophy is the precursor of Religion and Yoga. It is the higher intellectual process, which led Sages to question the nature and origin of their existence. Ancient Mystical Philosophy is a way to intellectually understand the process of existence, the reason for life, and the means to master it through intuitional wisdom. In this process of maturing consciousness, intellectual wisdom and knowledge gradually become intuitive. This process leads to greater and greater expansion of the mind and eventually to complete psychological liberation from worldly attachments. Thereby, one achieves a level of psychological experience, which is completely peaceful and transcendental. This lofty goal initially inspired Sages and Saints of ancient times to use symbols and myths to express these ideas. Later on whole bodies of mythical literature were developed to further express and elaborate these ideas. This became the basis for religious myths and spiritual scriptures. Eventually they created more detailed literature to intellectually explain the myths and symbols. These came to be known as secret (mystery) writings and Holy Scriptures. The first of these writings were the Ancient Egyptian hieroglyphs.

While it is true that yogic practices are used in religion, strictly speaking, yoga is neither a religion nor a philosophy. It should be thought of more as a way of life or discipline for promoting greater fullness and experience of life, physically, mentally and spiritually. Yoga was developed at the dawn of history by those who wanted more out of life. These special men and women wanted to discover the true origins of creation and of themselves. Therefore, they set out to explore the vast reaches of consciousness within themselves. They are sometimes referred to as "Seers," "Sages," "Saints," etc. Awareness or consciousness can only be increased when the mind is in a state of peace and harmony. Thus, the disciplines of devotion to the higher Self, meditation, right action and study of the wisdom teachings (which are all part of Yoga) are the primary means to controlling the mind and allowing the individual to mature psychologically and spiritually.

In contrast to the modern higher education system of the present, which develops a person's intellectual capacity, the early teachers (Sages) of the first places of learning (temple-universities) presented their teachings in a holistic manner. They were careful to maintain the balance in the educational system between the intellectual development and the spiritual evolution of every human being with which they had contact.

These teachings are the writings of Masters, those who were able to control their minds and bodies in such a way as to ascend to great psychological and psychic heights. Spiritual teaching is usually handed down from teacher to student, in a tradition, which spans thousands of years. These teachers or "seers" attained higher levels of communion with Cosmic Intelligence, the Pure Consciousness which underlies all things and then imparted their understanding of this state of consciousness and the means for attaining it to their disciples. Upon realizing this state, these spiritual masters discovered the nature of their own existence and the fact that they, along with the rest of humanity, nature and the universe, are one with that ultimate reality. The Sages realized that even though there are many names and forms in creation, all that can be seen is not only a part of God, the all-encompassing being, but in effect, is God. Nothing else really exists. All is one in God.

In ancient times, priests and priestesses underwent a process of instruction in various sciences (math, business, medical science, government, law, religion and yoga). Their studies could last up to 40 years or an entire lifetime. The Sages came back from the lofty heights of their spiritual achievements to manage society in accordance with righteous principles and spiritual ideals to assist others in attaining the beatific visions and the ever-present peace that cannot be disturbed by worldly occurrences: Spiritual Enlightenment. Thus, spiritual enlightenment is not just for the temple but for society as a whole. However, in order for this ideal to be possible, the leaders of society must be Sages, trained in the art and practice of Yoga. The Sages said that the heights they attained were obtainable by all human beings who possess the desire, will and knowledge to pursue and understand the truth of their inner being. This truth is not in books, but in the innermost heart of every human being. Maatian philosophy allows a person to discover the innermost core of all truth, the Higher Self within.

The text below the precepts from the Pert em Heru come from the Wisdom Texts, the writings of the Ancient Egyptian Sages. The writings of five recognized Ancient Egyptian Sages will be used to assist our studies of the 42 Precepts of Maat. Their names are Sage Merikara (c. 2,135-2,040 B.C.E.), * Sage Amenemope (c. 1,500-1,200 B.C.E), * Sage Ani (1,500 B.C.E.), * Sage Ptahotep (c. 2,300-2,150 B.C.E.)* and Sage Kaqemna (c. 2,575-2,465 B.C.E.). * The name of the Sage to whom the text is attributed, is given above the text in bold letters and underlined. Each of the exerpts have been edited and selected by Dr. Muata Ashby in accordance with their relation to the precepts they follow.

*The preceding dates are approximations. They represent the approximate date in which the religious precepts were first codified. Archeological and sociological history suggest that all of these systems undoubtedly existed for a long time before actually being "written down." The dates used above are the traditional dates used by the Egyptological establishments. However, due to errors in the process of figuring the dates of the life-spans of the average person in dynastic times the figures should be doubled in order to reflect a more realistic dating in accordance with the *Palermo Stone, Royal Tablets at Abydos, Royal Papyrus of Turin,* the *Dynastic List* of Manetho, listed below.

The history of Egypt begins in ancient times. It includes the Dynastic Period, the Hellenistic Period, Roman and Byzantine Rule (30 B.C.E.-638 A.C.E.), the Caliphate and the Mamalukes (642-1517 A.C.E.), Ottoman Domination (1082-1882 A.C.E.), and British colonialism (1882-1952 A.C.E.) as well as modern, independent Egypt (1952-). Ancient Egypt or Kamit is a civilization that flourished in Northeast Africa along the Nile River from before 5,500 B.C.E. until 30 B.C.E. In 30 B.C.E. Octavian (who was later known as the Roman Emperor, Augustus) put the last Egyptian King, Ptolemy XIV, a Greek ruler, to death. After this Egypt was formally annexed to Rome. Egyptologists normally divide Ancient Egyptian history into periods: The Early Dynastic Period (3,200-2,575 B.C.E.); The Old Kingdom or Old Empire (2,575-2,134 B.C.E.); the First Intermediate Period (2,134-2,040 B.C.E.); the Middle Kingdom or Middle Empire (2,040-1,640 B.C.E.); The Second Intermediate Period (1,640-1,532 B.C.E.); the New Kingdom or New Empire (1,550-1,070 B.C.E.); the third Intermediate Period (1,070-712 B.C.E.); the Late Period (712-332 B.C.E.); the Nubian Dynasty (712-657 B.C.E.); the Persian Dynasty (525-404 B.C.E.); the Native Revolt and re-establishment of Egyptian rule by Egyptians (404-343 B.C.E.); the Second Persian Period (343-332 B.C.E.); the Greco-Roman Period (332 B.C.E.-395 A.C.E.); the Byzantine Period[4] (395-640 A.C.E) and the Arab Conquest Period (640 A.C.E.). The individual dynasties are numbered, generally in Roman numerals, from I through XXX. The period after the New Kingdom saw greatness in culture and architecture under the rulership of Rameses II. However, after his rule, Egypt saw a decline from which it would never recover. This is the period of the downfall of Ancient Egyptian culture in which the Libyans ruled after The Tanite (or XXI) Dynasty. This was followed by the Nubian conquerors that founded the XXII dynasty and tried to restore Egypt to her past glory. However, having been weakened by the social and political turmoil of wars, Ancient Egypt fell to the Persians once more. The Persians conquered the country until the Greeks, under Alexander,

[4] Eastern Roman Empire after the break from Rome.

conquered them. The Romans followed the Greeks, and finally the Arabs conquered the land of Egypt in 640 A.C.E to the present.

However, the history, which has been classified above, is only the history of the "Dynastic Period." It reflects the view of traditional Egyptologists who have refused to accept the evidence of a predynastic period in Ancient Egyptian history contained in Ancient Egyptian documents such as the *Palermo Stone, Royal Tablets at Abydos, Royal Papyrus of Turin,* the *Dynastic List* of Manetho and the eye-witness accounts of Greek historians Herodotus (c. 484-425 B.C.E.) and Diodorus (Greek historian died about 20 B.C.E.). These sources speak clearly of a predynastic society, which stretches far into antiquity. The Dynastic period is what most people think of whenever Ancient Egypt is mentioned. This period is when the pharaohs (kings) ruled. The latter part of the Dynastic Period is when the Biblical story of Moses, Joseph, Abraham, etc., occurs (c. 2100? -1,000? B.C.E).[5] Therefore, those with a Christian background generally only have an idea about Ancient Egypt as it is related in the Bible. Although this biblical notion is very limited in scope, the significant impact of Ancient Egypt on Hebrew and Christian culture is evident even from the biblical scriptures. Actually, Egypt existed much earlier than most traditional Egyptologists are prepared to admit. The new archeological evidence related to the great Sphinx monument on the Giza Plateau and the ancient writings by Manetho, one of the last High Priests of Ancient Egypt, show that Ancient Egyptian history begins earlier than 10,000 B.C.E. and may date back to as early as 30,000-50,000 B.C.E.

The early Egyptologists assigned much older dated to the Dynastic Periods of Ancient Egypt. In more modern times these have been changed with little scientific evidence to support the change. The date for Mena, the first king of the first dynastic period (Old Kingdom) was given by Champollion at 5,867 B.C.E., by Mariette at 5,004 B.C.E., by Lepsius at 5,892 B.C.E., and by Brugsch at 4,455 B.C.E. for an average of 5,304.5 B.C.E. Modern Egyptologists have tried to calculate this date as 3,200 B.C.E. at the earliest. It is known that the Pharaonic (royal) calendar was in use by 4,240 B.C.E. This certainly required extensive astronomical skills and time for observation. Therefore, the history of Kamit (Egypt) must be reckoned to be extremely ancient. Thus, in order to grasp the antiquity of Ancient Egyptian culture, religion and philosophy, we will briefly review the history presented by the Ancient Egyptian Priest Manetho and some Greek Historians.

[5] Outside of the Bible there is no evidence of the birth of Abraham, Joseph, Moses, etc. Therefore, the dates are uncertain.

DEDICATION

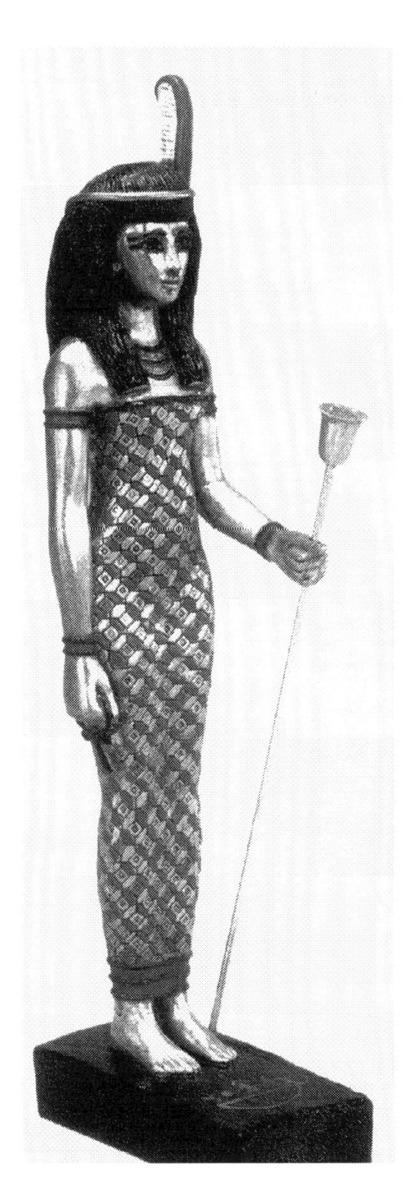

To
Goddess Maat
May her wisdom, compassion and glory ever shine always and everywhere as the sun which she beacons and leads!
And
The Sages of Sema Tawi (Ancient Egyptian Yoga):
Who codified and espoused the teachings and allowed this volume to be possible.

PRINCIPLE OF TRUTH

(1) "I have not done iniquity (what is wrong)." Variant: Acting with falsehood.

Sage Ptahotep

(5) If you are a man who leads,
Who controls the affairs of the many,
Seek out every beneficent deed,
See that your conduct is blameless.
Great is Maat, lasting in effect, Unchallenged since the time of Asar. One punishes the transgressor of laws, Though the greedy overlooks this;
Baseness may seize riches,
Yet crime never lands its wares;
In the end it is Maat that lasts,
Man says: "It is my father's ground.""

(6) "I have not defrauded offerings." Variant: or destroyed food supplies or increased or decreased the measures to profit.

Sage Amenemope

(12) Do not falsify the temple rations,
Do not be greedy and you'll find profit.

(17) Do not move the markers on the borders of fields,
Nor shift the position of the measuring-cord.
Do not be greedy for a cubit of land,
(18) Nor encroach on the boundaries of a widow.
The trodden path worn down by time,
He who disguises it in the fields,
When he has snared (it) by false oaths,
(19) He will be caught by the might of the Moon.
Recognize him who does this on earth: He is an oppressor of the weak,
A foe bent on destroying your being,
The taking of life is in his eye.
(20) His house is an enemy to the town,
His storage bins will be destroyed;
His wealth will be seized from his children's hands,
His possessions will be given to another.
Beware of destroying the borders of fields,
(21) Lest a terror carry you away;
One pleases God with the might of the lord
When one discerns the borders of fields.

Study Notes:

Desire your being to be sound,
Beware of Nebercher (Neberdjer), the Lord of All;
(22) Do not erase another's marker,
It profits you to keep it sound.
Plow your fields and you'll find what you need,
You'll receive bread from your threshing-floor.
(23) Better is a bushel given you by The God,
Than thousands through wrongdoing.

(54) Do not move the scales nor alter the weights,
Nor diminish the fractions of Measure;
(55) Do not desire a measure of the fields, Nor neglect those of the treasury.
The Ape[6] sits by the balance,
His heart is in the plummet;
Where is a god as great as Djehuti,
Who invented these things and made them?[7]
(56) Do not make for yourself deficient weights,
(57) They [the unrighteous liars, schemers, etc] are rich in grief through the might of God.
If you see someone who cheats, Keep your distance from him.

(9) "I have told no lies."

Sage Merikara

(11) Speak truth in your house,
That the officials of the land may respect you; Uprightness befits the lord,
The front of the house puts fear in the back.

Sage Amenemope

(41) Do not speak falsely to a man,
The God abhors it.
Do not sever your heart from your tongue,
That all your strivings may succeed.
You will be weighty before the others,
And secure in the hand of The God.
God hates the falsifier of words,
He greatly abhors the dissembler

(58) Do not covet copper,
Disdain beautiful linen;
What good is one dressed in finery,
If he cheats before The God?

[6] The God Djehuti, the determiner of the judgement of the soul in accordance with its actions in life.
[7] See the book The Ausarian Resurrection, to see how he instituted Maat in creation in accordance with the command of Ra.

Study Notes:

Faience disguised as gold,
Comes day, it turns to lead.

(66) Truth is the great support of God (or throne-bearer).

(67) Do not go to court before an official
In order to falsify your words;
(68) Do not vacillate in your answers,
When your witnesses accuse.
Do not strain (with) oaths by your lord,
(With) speeches at the hearing;
Tell the truth before the official,
(69) Lest he lay a hand on you.
If another day you come before him,
He will incline to all you say;
He will relate your speech to the Council of Thirty,
It will be observed on another occasion.

Sage Ani

Guard against the crime of fraud,
Against words that are not true;
Conquer malice in yourself.

(7) "I have not acted deceitfully." Variant: With crookedness.

Sage Amenemope

(30) Set your goodness before people,
Then you are greeted by all;
One welcomes the Uraeus, Approve what is good,
Spits upon Apophis, what is bad.

(45) Do not converse with a heated man,
So as to befriend a hostile, man.
If you are sent to transport straw,
Stay away from its container.
If a man is observed on a fraudulent errand,
He will not be sent on another occasion.[8]

(57) They [the unrighteous liars, schemers, etc] are rich in grief through the might of God.
If you see someone who cheats,
Keep your distance from him.

[8] Similar to the Bible injunction: Abstain from appearance of evil – 1 Thessalonians 5:22.

Study Notes:

(60) A measurer who indulges in cheating,
His Eye seals (the verdict) against him.

Sage Meri-ka-ra

The one who has wealth at home will not be partial,
He is a just man who lacks nothing.
The poor man does not speak justly,
Not righteous is one, who says, "I wish I had,"

Sage Ptahotep

10. If you are poor, serve a man of worth,
That all your conduct may be well with The God.[9]
Do not recall if he once was poor,
Don't be arrogant toward him
For knowing his former state;
Respect him for what has accrued to him,
For wealth does not come by itself.
It is their law for him whom they love,"'
His gain, he gathered it himself;
It is The God who makes him worthy
And protects him while he sleeps.
28. If you are a magistrate of standing,
Commissioned to satisfy the many,
Follow a straight line.
When you speak don't lean to one side,
Beware lest one complain:
"Judges, he distorts the matter!"
And your deed turns into a judgment (of you).
(Epilog) If a good example is set by him who leads,
He will be beneficent forever,[10]
His wisdom being for all time.
The wise feeds his ba[11] with what endures,
So that it is happy with him on earth.
The wise is known by his wisdom,
The great by his good actions;
His heart matches his tongue,
His lips are straight when he speaks; He has eyes that see,
His ears are made to hear what will profit his son,
Acting with truth he is free of falsehood.[12]

---

[9] The use of the term *Pa Neter* or The God, implies Supreme Being, above all *neteru* or gods and goddesses.
[10] Similar to the Indian Bhagavad Gita--Chapter 3 Karma Yogah--The Yoga of Action Verse 21 *Whatever a great man does, the same is followed by others. Whatever he sets as an example, the same the world emulates.*
[11] Eternal soul of a human being.
[12] Compare to Bhagavad Gita: Chapter 18 Moksha Sanyas Yogah--The Yoga of Renunciation and Liberation Verse 71 *Those who are endowed with faith and free of jealousy, they even on hearing this will become free of sins, and will attain to the higher worlds--those that are attained by men of meritorious deeds.*

Study Notes:

(24) "I have not stopped my ears against the words of right and wrong (Maat)."

Sage Ani

One will do all you say
If you are versed in writings;
Study the writings; put them in your heart,
Then all your words will be effective.

Sage Amenemope

(1) Give your ears, hear the sayings,
Give your heart to understand them;
It is an advantage to put them in your heart,
If you neglect them you will suffer!
Let them rest in the container of your belly,
May they be bolted in your heart;
(2) When there rises a whirlwind of words,
They'll be a mooring post for your tongue, a guide.
If you make your life with these in your heart, You will find it success and safety;
You will find my words a storehouse for life; Your being will prosper while upon earth.

(66) Keep firm your heart, steady your heart,
Say not, Evil should not be permitted to exist there is neither good nor evil in the hand of The God.
A man's tongue may be his steersman, but it is Nebertcher (i.e. The God) who is the pilot.

(99) The pilot who is watchful and alert to what is coming,
He will not wreck his boat.

Sage Meri-ka-ra

(28) The Lord of the Two Shores is one, who knows,
A king who has courtiers is not ignorant;
As one wise did he come from the womb…

Study Notes:

THE PRINCIPLE OF NON-VIOLENCE

(3) "I have not done violence (To anyone or anything)." Variant: Rapacious (Taking by force; plundering.)

Sage Meri-ka-ra

(28) For it is evil to destroy,
Difficult to restore what one has damaged,
To rebuild what one has demolished.
Beware of it! An action is repaid by its like,
And to every action there is a consequence (response-opposite reaction).

(2) "I have not robbed with violence."
(5) "I have not murdered man or woman." Variant: Or ordered someone else to commit murder.

Sage Meri-ka-ra

Beware of punishing unjustly,
Do not kill anyone, it does not serve you or bring what you desire.
Punish instead with beatings, and detention,
By these actions the land will be well ordered;
Except for the unrighteous one whose plans are found out...

(12) "I have attacked no one."

Sage Meri-ka-ra

(24) But this should be said to the Bowman:
Lo, the miserable Asiatic,
He is wretched because of the place he lives in:
Short of water, bare of wood,
Its paths are many and painful because of mountains.
He is nomadic, not dwelling in one place,
The constant need for food propels his legs,
He makes war since the time of Heru,
He is not successful in conquering nor is he conquered,
He is traitorous and does not announce the day of combat,
He is like a thief who darts around a group.
But as I live and shall be what I am,
When the Bowmen were a sealed wall,
I broke through their defenses,
I attack them with the forces from Lower Egypt,
I captured their men and women,
I took their cattle,
Until the Asiatics despised Egypt.
Do not worry about the Asiatic,

Study Notes:

The Asiatic is like a crocodile on its shore,
It snatches from a lonely road,
But it cannot capture anything from a populous town.

Sage Amenemope

(3) Don't create a disturbance or an outburst against the one, who attacks you,
Also, do not answer him or attack him yourself.
Whoever does evil will be rejected by the shore,
Its floodwater carries them away.
The Northwind comes to stop their unrighteousness,
(4) It mixes with the thunderstorm.
The storm cloud is large, and the crocodiles are vicious,
You heated man how are you now?
He cries out, and his voice reaches the heavens,
But it is the Moon who declares his crime.

From Pert em Heru Asar Ani Chapter 17

"I remove the thunder-cloud from the sky when there is a storm with thunder and lightning therein."
What is this?
"This storm was the raging of Ra at the thunder-cloud which [Set] sent forth against the Right Eye of Ra (the Sun). Djehuti removed the thunder- cloud from the Eye of Ra, and brought back the Eye living, healthy, sound, and with no defect in it to its owner. "Others, however, say that the thunder-cloud is caused by sickness in the Eye of Ra, which weepeth for its companion Eye (the Moon); at this time Djehuti cleanseth the Right Eye of Ra. "I behold Ra who was born yesterday from the thighs of the goddess Mehurt; his strength is my strength, and my strength is his strength."

(25) "I have not stirred up strife (disturbance)." "I have not caused terror." "I have not struck fear into any man."

Sage Amenemope

(73) *A* great gift of God, is Maat.
Given, it is, only to those chosen by God.
(74) The might of those who resemble God,
The poor are saved from their tormentor through it.

Sage Kaqemna

Do not cause terror in men and women; it is in opposition to The God.

Study Notes:

(26) "I have not caused any one to weep." Variant: Hoodwinked.

Sage Meri-ka-ra

(12) You will endure on earth when you do justice;
Calm those who weep, don't oppress the widow who is grieving,
Don't drive out a man from the property of his father;
Don't decrease the nobles in their possessions.

Sage Amenemope

(51) Do what is good and then you will prosper,
Do not dip your pen to injure a man.
The finger of the scribe[13] is the beak of the Ibis,
Beware of using it wrongly.
(91) Beware of neglecting the heart of man, it is a gift of God.

Sage Ptahotep

A good hearing soothes the heart.

Sage Amenemope cont.

(93) Do not make fun of a blind man,
Do not tease the dwarf,
Do not cause any hardship for those who are lame.
Don't taunt a man who is in the hand of The God,
Nor be vexed with him for any of his failings.
(94) Human beings are made of straw and clay,
The God is their fashioner.
It is God who destroys and creates daily,
It is God who makes a thousand people to be poor by his will,
Likewise, it is the same God who makes a thousand men into rulers,
When he is in his hour of life.
(95) Happy is the one, who reaches the beautiful west,[14]
When they are safe in the hand of The God.
(104) Do not revile or assail on a widow when you find her in the fields, which are not her, own,
And then fail to be patient with her reply.

---

[13] The god Djehuti.
[14] Amentet, the final abode of blessed (Enlightened) souls.

Study Notes:

Sage Ptahotep

6. Do not scheme against people, God punishes accordingly:
If a man says: "I shall live by scheming,"
He will lack bread for his mouth.
If a man says: "I shall be rich,"
He will have to say: "My cleverness has snared me."
If he says: "I will snare for myself,"
He will be unable to say: "I snared for my profit.
If a man says: "I will rob someone,"
He will end being given to a stranger.
People's schemes do not prevail,
God's command is what prevails;
Live then in the midst of peace,
What they give comes by itself.

(28) "I have not avenged myself." Variant: Resentment.

Sage Amenemope

(78) Do not say: "Find me a strong superior,
For a man in your town has injured me";
Do not say: "Find me a protector, For one who hates me has injured me."
(79) Indeed you do not know the plans of God,
And should not weep for tomorrow;
Settle in the arms of The God,
Your silence will overthrow them (the wrongdoers).
(80) The crocodile that makes no sound,
Dread of it is ancient.
(81) Do not empty your belly to everyone, And thus destroy respect of you;
Broadcast not your words to others,
Nor join with one who bares his heart.
(82) Better is one whose speech is in his belly,
Than he who tells it to cause harm.
(84) Do not provoke your adversary,
So as to (make) him tell his thoughts;
Do not leap to come before him,
When you do not see his doings.
First gain insight from his answer,
Then keep still and you will succeed.
(85) Leave it to him to empty his belly,
Know how to sleep, he will be found out.
Do not harm him,
(86) Be wary of him, do not ignore him. Indeed you do not know the plans of God,
And should not weep for tomorrow;
(87) Settle in the arms of The God,
Your silence will overthrow them.

Study Notes:

(30) "I have not acted insolently or with violence."
(34) "I have not done harm or evil." Variant: Thought evil.

Sage Meri-ka-ra

Don't act with evil, kindness is an expression of good nature,
Make your memory last through love of you.
Increase the [people], befriend the town,
God will be praised for (your) donations

Sage Ptahotep

19. If you want a perfect conduct,
To be free from every evil,
Guard against the vice of greed:
A grievous sickness without cure,
There is no treatment for it.
It embroils fathers, mothers,
And brothers of the mother,
It parts wife from husband;
It is a compound of all evils,
A bundle of all hateful things.
That man endures whose rule is righteousness,
Who walks a straight line;
He will make a will by it,
The greedy has no tomb.

THE PRINCIPLE OF NON-STEALING

(4) "I have not committed theft." Variant: I have not Coveted.

Sage Meri-ka-ra

(8) Make people come [to you] through your good nature,
A wretch is the one who desires the land [of his neighbor],
A fool is the one who covets what others possess.

Sage Amenemope

(23) Possessions and wealth gained wrongly stay not a day in bin and barn,
They make no food for the beer jar;
A moment is their stay in the granary,
If thou sailest with a thief thou wilt be left in the river.

(28) Do not rejoice in wealth from theft,
Nor complain of being poor.

Study Notes:

If the leading archer presses forward,
His company abandons him;
(29) The boat of the greedy is left (in) the mud,
While the bark of the silent sails with the wind. Get into the habit of praying sincerely to Aten (i.e. the solar Disk) as he rises in the sky,
Saying: "Grant me strength, well-being and health";
He will give you your needs for this life,
And you will be safe from fear.

(8) "I have not robbed the things that belong to God." Variant: Or the offerings to the dead.

Sage Amenemope

(12) Do not falsify the temple rations,
Do not be greedy and you'll find profit.
Do not remove a servant of The God,
So as to do favors to another.
(13) Do not say: "Today is like tomorrow, How will this end?
(14) Comes tomorrow, today has vanished,
The deep has become the water's edge. Crocodiles are bared, hippopotami stranded, The fish crowded together.

(76) Don't falsify the oracles in the scrolls, And thus disturb the plans of God;
(77) Don't use for yourself the might of God, As if there were no Fate and Destiny.
Hand over property to its owners,
Thus do you seek life for yourself;
Don't raise your desire in their house,
Or your bones belong to the execution-block.

Sage Meri-ka-ra

(27) He who is silent toward violence diminishes the offerings.

Sage Amenemope

(15) Jackals are sated; birds are in feast,
The fishnets have been drained.
But all the silent in the temple,
They say: "Ra's blessing is great."
Cling to the silent, then you find life,
(16) Your being will prosper upon earth.

Study Notes:

(10) "I have not snatched away food." Variant: food that belongs to the child.

SHARING ALIKE

Sage Amenemope

(5) Steer, we will ferry the wicked,
We do not act like his kind;
Lift him up; give him your hand,
Leave him (in) the hands of The God;
(6) Fill his belly with bread of your own; give him drink, for it is in the heart of the God to show another act of compassion,
That he be sated and weep.

Sage Ptahotep

34. Be generous as long as you live,
What leaves the storehouse does not return;
It is the food to be shared which is coveted,
One whose belly is empty is an accuser;
One deprived becomes an opponent,
Don't have him for a neighbor.
Kindness is a man's memorial
For the years after the function.
35- Know your helpers, then you prosper, Don't be mean toward your friends,
They are one's watered field,
And greater then one's riches,
For what belongs to one belongs to another.
The character of a son-of-man is profit to him; Good nature is a memorial.

Sage Ani

Do not eat bread while another stands by
Without extending your hand to him.
As to food, it is here always,
It is man who does not last;

One man is rich, another is poor,
But food remains for him who shares it.
As to him who was rich last year,
He is a vagabond this year;
Don't be greedy to fill your belly,
You don't know your end at all.
Should you come to be in want,
Another may do good to you.
When last year's watercourse is gone,
Another river is here today;

Study Notes:

Great lakes become dry places,
Sandbanks turn into depths.
Man does not have a single way,
The lord of life confounds him."

Sage Meri-ka-ra

(23) When free men are given land,
They work for you like a single team;
No rebel will arise among them,
And Hapi will not fail to come.
The dues of the Northland are in your hand,
For the mooring-post is staked in the district I made in the East
From Hebenu to Heruway;
It is settled with towns, filled with people,
Of the best in the whole land,
To repel attacks against them.
May I see a brave man who will copy it,
Who will add to what I have done,
A wretched heir would disgrace me.

(41) "I have never magnified my condition beyond what was fitting or increased my wealth, except with such things as are (justly) mine own possessions by means of Maat." Variant: I have not disputed over possessions except when they concern my own rightful possessions. Variant: I have not desired more than what is rightfully mine.

"They who revere MAAT are long lived;
they who are covetous have no tomb."

–Ancient Egyptian Proverb

Sage Amenemope

On Contentment:

(23) The beggar in God's hand is better off than the rich man in his palace.
Crusts of bread and a loving heart are better than rich food and mental agitation.
Hanker therefore after daintiness.[15]
Mind thy business, and let every man do his when he wishes to do it.
Learn to be content with what thou hast.
(24) Better is poverty in the hand of The God, Than -wealth in the storehouse;
Better is bread with a happy heart,
Than wealth with vexation.
(25) Do not set your heart on wealth,
There is no ignoring Fate and Destiny;
Do not let your heart go straying,
Every man comes to his hour.

[15] That which is delicately beautiful or charming; exquisite. delicious or choice, of refined taste; discriminating values.

Study Notes:

Do not strain to seek increase,
(26) What you have, let it suffice you.
If riches come to you by theft,
They will not stay the night with you.
Comes day they are not in your house,
Their place is seen but they are not there;
(27) Earth opened its mouth, leveled them, swallowed them,
And made them sink into the deep.
They made a hole as big as their size,
And sank into the netherworld;
They made themselves wings like geese,
And flew away to the sky.

(42) Do not covet a poor man's goods,
Nor hunger for his bread;
A poor man's goods are a block in the throat,
It makes the gullet vomit.
He who makes gain by lying oaths,
His heart is misled by his belly;
Where there is fraud success is feeble,
The bad spoils the good.
You will be guilty before your superior,
And confused in your account;
Your pleas will be answered by a curse,
Your prostrations by a beating.
The big mouthful of bread-you swallow, you vomit it,
And you are emptied of your gain.

(44) Do not desire a noble's wealth,
Nor make free with a big mouthful of bread;
If he sets you to manage his property,
Shun his, and yours will prosper.

Sage Ptahotep

14- If you are among the people,
Gain supporters through being trusted;
The trusted man who does not vent his belly's speech,
He will himself become a leader.
A man of means-what is he like?
Your name is good, you are not maligned,
Your body is sleek, your face benign,
One praises you without your knowing.
He whose heart obeys his belly
Puts contempt of himself in place of love,

Study Notes:

His heart is bald, his body unanointed;
The greathearted is God-given,
He who obeys his belly belongs to the enemy.

Sage Ani

Do not rely on another's goods (possessions),
Guard what you acquire yourself;
Do not depend on another's wealth,
Lest he become master in your house.
Build a house or find and buy one,
Shun contention
Don't say: "My mother's father has a house,
'A house that lasts,' one calls it;
When you come to share with your brothers,
Your portion may be a storeroom.
If your god lets you have children,
They'll say: "We are in our father's house."
Be a man hungry or sated in his house,
It is his walls that enclose him.
Do not be a mindless person,
Then your god will give you wealth.

Attend to your position,
Be it low or high;
It is not good to press forward,
Step according to rank.

Sage Meri-ka-ra

(30) Make firm your station in the graveyards,
By being upright, by doing justice,
Upon which men's hearts rely.
The loaf of the upright is preferred
To the ox of the evildoer.

Study Notes:

THE PRINCIPLE OF RIGHT ACTION-SELF-CONTROL

SELFLESS SERVICE

(29) "I have not worked grief, I have not abused anyone."

Sage Meri-ka-ra

God thinks of him who works for him.

Sage Ptahotep

35- Know your helpers, then you prosper, Don't be mean toward your friends,
They are one's watered field,
And greater then one's riches,
For what belongs to one belongs to another.
The character of a son-of-man is profit to him; Good nature is a memorial.

From Chapter 125 of The Book of Coming Forth By Day from Papyrus Nu

Live upon truth,
Feed upon truth,
Perform the ordinances of men,
and the things which gratify the gods.
Propitiate the God by doing his will,
Given bread to the hungry man,
and water to him that was athirst,
and apparel to the naked man,
and a ferry boat to he who has no boat…
–From the Ancient Egyptian Papyrus of Nu

I have not caused anyone to go hungry.

Sage Amenemope

Be kind to the poor.
Get thee a seat in the sanctuary.
Be strong to do the Will of God.
You will share in the offerings of your lord.
(32) When you're revered and your coffin conceals you,
You will be safe through the power of God."

(105) Do not refuse your oil jar to a stranger, Double it before your brothers.
(106) God prefers the person who honors the poor,
To the one who worships the wealthy.[16]
The love of God is better than the reverence of the nobleman.

[16] Similar to the Bible: Mark 8:36 For what shall it profit a man, if he shall gain the whole world, and lose his own soul?

Study Notes:

On Business and Commerse

Sage Amenemope

(48) Do not assess a man who has nothing,
And thus falsify your pen.
If you find a large debt against a poor man, Make it into three parts;
Forgive two, let one stand,
(49) You will find it a path of life.

(66) Haste not to be rich, but be not slothful in thine own interest.

(83) One does not run to reach success,
One does not move to spoil it.

(108) Don't make yourself a ferry on the river, And then strain to seek its fare;
(109) Take the fare from him who is wealthy,
And let pass him who is poor.

RIGHT ACTION

(1) "I have not done iniquity (what is wrong)." Variant: Acting with falsehood.

Sage Kaqemna

Satisfy your dependents by means of righteous deeds. This is what the favored ones of The God do.[17]

Sage Amenemope

Pass not thy day in beer-houses and over-eating or thou wilt become a mere mass of food.

Sage Ani

Don't indulge in drinking beer,
lest you utter evil speech
And don't know what you're saying.
If' you fall and hurt your body,
None holds out a hand to you;
Your companions in the drinking
Stand up saying: "Out with the drunk!"

[17] Similar to the Bhagavad Gita: Chapter 12 Bhakti Yogah--The Yoga of Devotion verse 20. *Those who are devoted to the Immortal Dharma set forth above,* endowed with faith, regarding Me as the Supreme, they—My Devotees are extremely dear to me.

Study Notes:

If one comes to seek you and talk with you.
One finds you lying on the ground,
As if you were a little child.

Sage Amenemope

(49) After sleep, Indulge not in morning slumber while the day breaks majestically in the sky.
What can be compared to dawn and daybreak for beauty?
To what can the man who knows not the dawn be compared?
For whilst God is performing His splendid work that man is wallowing in slothfulness.
Better is praise and love of men,
Than material wealth in your storehouse;
Better is bread with a happy heart,
Than wealth with vexation.

(20) "I have not committed any sin against my own purity."
(22) "I have not done that which is abominable."

Sage Amenemope

The liar is an abomination to him.

Sage Ani

God abhors shouting; (too much talking)

Sage Kaqemna

Beloved of The God is obedience; disobedience is an abomination to The God.

(15) "I have not laid waste the ploughed lands."
(36) "I have never befouled the water." Variant: held back the water from flowing in its season. I have not extinguished a fire when it should burn.

Form Pert em Heru Asar Nu

I have not stopped the water when it should flow. I have not made a cutting in a canal of running water.

Chapter 30B of the *Book of Coming Forth By Day* states:

This utterance (hekau) shall be recited by a person purified and washed; one who has not eaten animal flesh or fish.

Study Notes:

THE PRINCIPLE OF RIGHT SPEECH

(11) "I have not uttered evil words." Variant: Or allowed myself to become sullen, to sulk or to become depressed.

From A Hymn of Praise to Asar Un-Nefer.

Thou makest the Two Lands to flourish through Maak-heru (Truth-speaking), in the presence of him who is the Lord to the Uttermost Limit.

Sage Amenemope

(62) Do not lie down in fear of tomorrow:
"Comes day, how will tomorrow be?"
Man ignores how tomorrow will be;
God is ever in his perfection,
Man is ever in his failure.
(63) The words men say are one thing,
The deeds of The God are another.
Do not say: "I have done no wrong,"
And then strain to seek a quarrel;
The wrong belongs to The God...

Sage Kaqemna

Not known are the things that will do God.

(17) "I have not spoken against anyone (slander)." Variant: Babbled, gossiped.

Sage Ptahotep

23- Do not repeat calumny,
Nor should you listen to it,
It is the spouting of the hot-bellied.
Report a thing observed, not heard,
If it is negligible, don't say anything,
He who is before you recognizes worth.
'If a seizure is ordered and carried out,
Hatred will arise against him who seizes;
Calumny is like a dream against which one covers the face.

Do not malign anyone,
Great or small, the Ba abhors it.

Study Notes:

Sage Amenemope

(33) Do not shout "crime" against a man,
When the cause of (his) flight is hidden. Hide the flight of the runaway slave.
(34) Whether you hear something good or evil,
Do it outside where it is not heard.
Disregard what thou hearest, whether good or bad; it is not thy business, heed it not. Speak only what is good, what is bad hide in thy belly.

(47) Do not bear witness with false words,
So as to brush aside a man by your tongue.
(49) You will find it a path of life.

(100) Do not revile one, who is older than you,
He has seen Ra before you;
(101) Let there be no reason for him to report you to the Aten at his rising,
Saying: "A youth has reviled an old man."
Very painful before Pre,
Is a youth who reviles an elder.

(23) "I have not uttered fiery words. I have not been a man or woman of anger."

Sage Meri-ka-ra

(1) The hothead incites citizens; He creates divisions among the young; If you see that people follow him,
(2) Speak out against him before those who give council, Suppress the hothead, he is against harmony, The talker is a troublemaker for society. Your duty is to curb the multitude, and suppress its heat...

Sage Amenemope

(31) Guard your tongue from harmful speech,
Then you will be loved by others.
You will find your place in the Sanctuary, the House of God,

(35) Do not befriend the heated man,
Nor approach him for conversation. Avoid the scandalmonger.
His lips are datesyrup, his tongue is a deadly dagger, and a blazing fire is within him. Avoid converse with evil men, for that God hates. Make thy plans wisely. Be dignified. Place thyself for safety in the hand of God.

(37) Swift is the speech of one who is angered,
More than wind [over] water.
He tears down; he builds up with his tongue, When he makes his hurtful speech.

Study Notes:

THREE KINDS OF DISPUTANTS

Sage Ptahotep

2. If you meet a disputant in action,
A powerful man, superior to you,
Fold your arms; bend your back,
To flout him will not make him agree with you.
Make little of the evil speech
By not opposing him while he's in action;
He will be called an ignoramus,
Your self-control will match his pile (of words).

3- If you meet a disputant in action, who is your equal, on your level,
You will make your worth exceed his by silence,
While he is speaking evilly,
There will be much talk by the hearers,
Your name will be good in the minds of the magistrates.

4- If you meet a disputant in action,
A poor man, not your equal,
Do not attack him because he is weak,
Let him alone, he will confute himself.
Do not answer him to relieve your heart,
Do not vent yourself against your opponent,
Wretched is he, who injures a poor man,
O One will wish to do what you desire,
You will beat him through the magistrates reproof.

Sage Ptahotep

25- If you are mighty, gain respect through knowledge
And through gentleness of speech.
Don't command except as is fitting,
He who provokes gets into trouble.
Don't be haughty, lest you be humbled,
Don't be mute, lest you be chided.
When you answer one who is fuming,
Avert your face, control yourself.
The flame of the hot-heart sweeps across,
He who steps gently, his path is paved.
He who frets all day has no happy moment,
He who's gay all day can't keep house.

33- If you probe the character of a friend,
Don't inquire, but approach him,
Deal with him alone,

Study Notes:

So as not to suffer from his manner.
Dispute with him after a time,
Test his heart in conversation;
If what he has seen escapes him,
If he does a thing that annoys you,
Be yet friendly with him, don't attack;
Be restrained, don't let fly,
Don't answer with hostility,
Neither part from him nor attack him;
His time does not fail to come,
One does not escape what is fated.

Sage Ani

Do not speak rudely to a brawler,
When you are attacked hold yourself back;
You will find this good when your relations are friendly,
When trouble has come it will help you bear up,
And the aggressor will desist.
Deeds that are effective toward a stranger
Are very noxious to a brother."
Your people will hail you when you are joyful,
They will weep freely (when you are sad)';
When you are happy the brave look to you,
When you are lonely you find your relations.

Do not enter into a crowd,
If you find it in an uproar
And about to come to blows.
Don't pass anywhere near by,
Keep away from their tumult,
Lest you be brought before the court,
When an inquiry is made.
Stay away from hostile people,
Keep your heart quiet among fighters;
An outsider is not brought to court,
One who knows nothing is not bound in fetters.

In a quarrel do not speak,
Your silence will serve you well.

From the Pert em Heru Asar Nu

I have not known men who were of no account.

Study Notes:

(33) "I have not multiplied my speech overmuch." (Talk too much)

Sage Amenemope

(50) Do not recall yourself to a man,
Nor strain to seek his hand.
If he says to you: "Here is a gift."
[No poor person] will refuse it.
Don't blink at him, nor bow your head,
Nor turn aside your gaze.
Salute him with your mouth, say, "Greetings".
He will desist and you succeed.
Do not rebuff him in his approach,
[At another time he'll be taken away]

(89) Do not listen to an official's reply indoors
In order to repeat it to another outside.
(90) Do not let your word be carried outside,
Lest your heart be aggrieved.

Sage Ptahotep

8. If you are a man of trust,
Sent by one great man to another,
Adhere to the nature of him who sent you, Give his message as he said it.
Guard against reviling speech,
Which embroils one great with another;
Keep to the truth, don't exceed it,
But an outburst"' should not be repeated.

24- If you are a man of worth,
Who sits in his master's council,
Concentrate on excellence,
Your silence is better than chatter.
Speak when you know you have a solution,
It is the skilled who should speak in council;
Speaking is harder than all other work,
He who understands it makes it serve.

Sage Ani

Do not reveal your heart to a stranger,
He might use your words against you;
The noxious speech that came from your mouth,

Study Notes:

He repeats it and you make enemies.
A man may be ruined by his tongue,
Beware and you will do well."
A man's belly is wider than a granary,
And full of all kinds of answers;
(10) Choose the good one and say it,
While the bad is shut in your belly.
A rude answer brings a beating,
Speak sweetly and you will be loved.
Don't ever talk back to your attacker,
Do not set a trap (for him);
It is The God, who judges the righteous,
His fate comes and takes him away.

(35) "I have not worked treason or curses on the King."

Sage Ptahotep

29. If you are angered by a misdeed,
Lean toward a man on account of his rightness;
Pass it over, don't recall it,
Since he was silent to you the first day.

(37) "I have not spoken scornfully." Variant: Or yelled unnecessarily or raised my voice.

Sage Ptahotep

A quarreler is a mindless person,
If he is known as an aggressor
The hostile man will have trouble in the neighborhood.

Sage Ani

Conquer malice in your self,
A quarrelsome man does not rest on the morrow.
Keep away from a hostile man,
Do not let him be your comrade;
Befriend one, who is straight and true,
One whose actions you have seen.
If your rightness matches his,
The friendship will be balanced

Study Notes:

Sage Meri-ka-ra

(4) If you are skilled in the art of speech, you will prevail,
The tongue is [a leader or wise person's] sword;
Speaking rightly is more powerful than all fighting,
The skillful in speech (ethics-philosophy) cannot be overcome.

Sage Amenemope

(98) The arm is not hurt by being bared,
The back is not broken by bending it.
A man does not lose anything by speaking sweetly,
Nor does he gain anything if his speech is agitated and irate.
(99) The pilot who is watchful and alert to what is coming,
He will not wreck his boat.

THE PRINCIPLE OF RIGHT WORSHIP

(13) "I have not slaughtered the cattle that are set apart for the Gods." Variant: The Sacred bull - Apis)
(21) "I have not violated sacred times and seasons."

Sage Ani

Give thyself to the God,
Keep thyself daily for God and let tomorrow be as today.
Offer to your god,
Beware of offending him.
Do not question his images,
Do not accost him when he appears.
Do not jostle him in order to carry him,
Do not disturb the oracles."
Be careful; help to protect him,
Let your eye watch out for his wrath,
And kiss the ground in his name.
He gives power in a million forms,
He who magnifies him is magnified.
God of this earth is the sun in the sky,
While his images are on earth;
When incense is given them as daily food,
The lord of risings is satisfied.

Sage Meri ka ra

(9) A million men do not benefit the Lord of the Two Lands.
Is there [a man] who lives forever?
He who comes with Asar passes,

Study Notes:

He leaves those who indulged themselves.
(13) The *ba* comes to the place it knows,
It does not miss its former path,
No kind of magic holds it back,
It comes to those who give it water.

(27) Supply the offerings, revere The God,
Don't say, "it is trouble," don't slacken your hands.
(30) Work for God, He will work for you also,
With offerings that make the altar flourish,
With carvings that proclaim your name,
God thinks of him who works for him.

Sage Amenemope

(62) Do not lie down in fear of tomorrow:
"Comes day, how will tomorrow be?"
Man ignores how tomorrow will be;
God is ever in his perfection,
Man is ever in his failure.

Sage Kaqemna

The ability to eat bread is under the dispensation of The God.

(32) "I have not transgressed or angered God."

Sage Amenemope

(46) Do not cheat a man (through) pen on scroll,
The God abhors it...

(75) Do not make for yourself false documents,
They are a deadly provocation;
They (mean) the great restraining oath,
They, (mean) a hearing by the herald.
(76) Don't falsify the oracles in the scrolls,
And thus disturb the plans of God;
(77) Don't use for yourself the might of God,
As if there were no Fate and Destiny.
Hand over property to its owners,
Thus do you seek life for yourself;
Don't raise your desire in their house,
Or your bones belong to the execution-block.

Sage Meri-ka-ra

(14) The Court that judges the wretch,
You know they are not lenient,
On the day of judging the miserable,
In the hour of doing their task.
It is painful when the accuser has knowledge,
Do not trust in length of years,
They view a lifetime in an hour!
When a man remains over after death,
His deeds are set beside him as treasure,
And being yonder lasts forever.
A fool is who does what they reprove!
He who reaches them without having done wrong
Will exist there like a god,
Free-striding like the lords forever!

From Pert em Heru Asar Nu
I have not masturbated [in the sanctuaries of the god of my city].

Study Notes:

Sage Ani

The Art of Prayer.

Do not raise your voice in the House of God,
He abhors shouting; (too much talking)
Pray by yourself with a loving heart,
Who's every word is hidden.
He will grant your needs,
He will hear your words,
He will accept your offerings.

Sage Amenemope

(6) Another thing that is good in the heart of The God:
To pause before speaking.

> **(38) "I have not cursed The God." Variant: Or ignored The God. I have not turned back the god at his appearances.**

Sage Meri-ka-ra

(17) Make your monuments [worthy] of The God,
This keeps alive their maker's name,
A man should do what profits his *ba*.
In the monthly service, wear the white sandals,
Visit the temple, discover the mysteries,
Enter the shrine, eat bread in God's house;
Proffer libations, multiply the loaves,
Make ample the daily offerings,
It profits him who does it.
Endow your monuments according to your wealth,
Even one day of spiritual practice leads to eternity,
Even an hour contributes to the future,
God recognizes the one who works for Him.

Sage Ani

Offer to your god,
Beware of offending him.
Do not question his images,
Do not accost him when he appears.
Do not jostle him in order to carry him,
Do not disturb the oracles."
Be careful; help to protect him,
Let your eye watch out for his wrath,
And kiss the ground in his name.
He gives power in a million forms,
He who magnifies him is magnified.

Study Notes:

God of this earth is the sun in the sky,
While his images are on earth;
When incense is given them as daily food,
The lord of risings is satisfied.

From The Stele of Djehuti-Nefer:
"Consume pure foods and pure thoughts with pure hands, adore celestial beings, and become associated with wise ones: sages, saints and prophets; make offerings to GOD."

From pert Em Heru Asar Ani:
The Chapter of Entering the Hall of Maat shall be recited or chanted by the spiritual aspirant when he is cleansed and purified, and is arrayed in linen apparel, and is shod with sandals of white leather, and his eyes are painted with antimony, and his body is anointed with unguent made of myrrh.

(42) "I have never thought evil (blasphemed) or slighted the God in my native town." I have not [attempted] to direct servants [I have not belittled God].

Sage Meri-ka-ra

(5) The wise one is a [teacher] to the nobles.
Those who know that he knows will not attack him,
No [crime or injustice] occurs when a wise one is near; justice comes to them distilled,
In the form of the sayings of the ancestors.
Copy your fathers, your ancestors,
(6) See that the their wise words cndurc in books,
Open them and read them, copy their knowledge, they who are taught become skilled.
(30) One should revere The God on his path,
Made of costly stone, fashioned of bronze.
As watercourse is replaced by watercourse,
So no river allows itself to be concealed,
It breaks the channel in which it was hidden.
So also the *ba* goes to the place it knows,
And strays not from its former path.

THE PRINCIPLE OF BALANCE OF MIND - REASON - RIGHT THINKING

(14) "I have not eaten my heart" (overcome with anguish and distraught). Variant: Committed perjury.

Sage Amenemope

(39) The day he (angry person, angry speech) is charged with his crime
Is misfortune for his children.
If only Klmum (Knum) came to him,
The Potter to the heated man,
So as to knead the [defect in the] heart.
He is like a young wolf in the farmyard,

Study Notes:

He turns one eye against the other,
He causes brothers to quarrel.
He runs before every wind like clouds,
He dims the radiance of the sun;
He flips his tail like the crocodile's young,
His lips are sweet, his tongue is bitter,
A fire burns in his belly.
Don't leap to join such a one,
Lest a terror carry you away.
(40) Don't force yourself to greet the heated man,
For then you injure your own heart;
Do not say "greetings" to him falsely,
While there is terror in your belly.

Sage Ani

Do not talk back to an angry superior,
Let him have his way;
Speak sweetly when he speaks sourly,
It's the remedy that calms the heart.
Fighting answers carry sticks,
And your strength collapses;

Do not vex your heart.
He will return to praise you soon,
When his hour of rage, has passed.
If your words please the heart,
The heart tends to accept them;
Choose silence for yourself,

Submit to what he does.
Befriend the herald of your quarter,
Do not make him angry with you.
Give him food from your house,
Do not slight his requests;

Say to him, "Welcome, welcome here,"
No blame accrues to him who does it.

Sage Ptahotep

11. Follow your heart as long as you live.
Do no more than is required,
Do not shorten the time of "follow-the-heart,"
Trimming its moment offends the ka.
Don't waste time on daily cares

"To destroy an undesirable rate of mental vibration, concentrate on the opposite vibration to the one to be suppressed."
–Ancient Egyptian Proverb from the Kybalion

"Neither let prosperity put out the eyes of circumspection, nor abundance cut off the hands of frugality; they that too much indulge in the superfluities of life, shall live to lament the want of its necessaries."

"See that prosperity elate not thine heart above measure; neither adversity depress thine mind unto the depths, because fortune beareth hard against you. Their smiles are not stable, therefore build not thy confidence upon them; their frowns endure not forever, therefore let hope teach you patience."

–Ancient Egyptian Proverbs

Study Notes:

Beyond providing for your household;
When wealth has come, follow your heart,
Wealth does no good if one is glum!

Sage Ani

He who is slack amounts to nothing,
Honored is the man who's active.

(16) "I have not been an eavesdropper or pried into matters to make mischief." Variant: Spy.

Sage Ani

Do not enter the house of anyone,
Until he admits you and greets you;
Do not snoop around in his house; let your eye observe in silence.
Do not speak of him to another outside,
Who was not with you;
A great deadly crime this is.

(18) "I have not allowed myself to become angry without cause." Variant: Not adopted a quarrelsome nature.

Sage Amenemope

(7) Don't start a quarrel with a hot-mouthed man,
Nor needle him with words.
Pause before a foe; bend before an attacker,
Sleep (meditate on it) before speaking.
A storm that bursts like fire in straw,
(8) Such is the heated man in his hour.
Withdraw from him, leave him alone,
The God knows how to answer him.
If you make your life with these (words) in your heart,
Your children will observe them.
(9) As for the heated man in the temple,
He is like a tree growing [indoors];
A moment lasts its growth of [shoots]
Its end comes about in the woodshed;
(10) It is floated far from its place,
The flame is its burial shroud.

Matthew 6:16-17

Ye shall know them by their fruits. Do men gather grapes from thorns, or figs from thistles?
Even so every good tree bringeth forth good fruit; but a corrupt tree bringeth forth bad fruit.

Matthew 3:10

And now also the axe is laid to the root of the trees: therefore every tree which bringeth not forth good fruit is hewn down, and cast into the fire.

Study Notes:

The truly silent, who keeps apart,
He is like a tree grown in a meadow.
It greens; it doubles its yield,
(11) It stands in front, of its lord.
Its fruit is sweet, its shade delightful,
Its end comes in the garden.

(66) Keep firm your heart, steady your heart,
Say not, "Evil should not be permitted to exist"; there is neither good nor evil in the hand of the God.

(31) "I have not judged hastily." Variant: or been impatient.

Sage Meri-ka-ra

(3) May you be justified before The God;
That a man may say of you even when you are absent,
That you punish in accordance [with what is just for the crime].
Good nature allows a man to experience heaven,
The cursing of the [angry and agitated ones] is painful to oneself.

(16) Do not prefer the well born to the commoner,
Choose a man on account of his skills,
Then all crafts are done --- . . .

Sage Amenemope

(33) Do not shout "crime" against a man,
When the cause of (his) flight is hidden.

(71) Do not incline to-the well-dressed man,
And rebuff the one in rags.
(72) Don't accept the gift of a powerful man,
And deprive the weak for his sake.

Sage Ptahotep

12. If you are a man of worth
And produce a son by the grace of god,
If he is straight takes after you,
Takes good care of your possessions,
Do for him all that is good,
He is your son; your ka begot him,
Don't withdraw your heart from him.

Study Notes:

But an offspring can make trouble:
If he strays, neglects your counsel,
Disobeys all that is said,
His mouth spouting evil speech,
Punish him for all his talk.
They hate him, who crosses you,
His guilt was fated in the womb;
He whom they guide can not go wrong,
Whom they make boatless can not cross.

17- If you are a man who leads,
Listen calmly to the speech of one who pleads;
Don't stop him from purging his body
Of that which he planned to tell.
A man in distress wants to pour out his heart more than that his case be won.
About him who stops a plea
One says: "Why does he reject it?"
Not all one pleads for can be granted,
But a good hearing soothes the heart.

36. Punish firmly, chastise soundly,
Then repression of crime becomes an example;
Punishment except for crime
Turns the complainer into an enemy.

(39) "I have not behaved with arrogance." Variant: Boastful.
(40) "I have not been overwhelmingly proud or sought for distinctions for myself (Selfishness)."

Sage Amenemope

(107) When you are given an oar in the midst of the deep,
Bend your arms and take it.
The God will not be offended thereby.

Sage Ptahotep

1. Don't be proud of your knowledge,
Consult the ignorant and the wise;
The limits of art are not reached,
No artist's skills are perfect;
Good speech is more hidden than grindstone,
Yet may be found among workers at the grindstones.

9. If you plow and there's growth in the field,
And god lets it prosper in your hand,
Do not boast at your neighbors' side,

Study Notes:

One has great respect for the silent man:
Man of character is man of wealth.
If he robs he is like a crocodile in court.
Don't impose on one, who is childless,
Neither decry nor boast of it;
There is many a father who has grief,
And a mother of children less content than another;
It is the lonely whom god fosters,
While the family man prays for a follower.

30- If you are great after having been humble,
Have gained wealth after having been poor,
In the past, in a town which you know,
Knowing your former condition,
Do not put trust in your wealth,
Which came to you as gift of god;
So that you will not fall behind one like you,
To whom the same has happened.

Sage Ani

Attend to your position,
Be it low or high;
It is not good to press forward,
Step according to rank.
Do not intrude on a man in his house,
Enter when you have been called;
He may say "Welcome" with his mouth,
Yet deride you in his thoughts.
One gives food to one, who is hated,
Supplies to one who enters uninvited.
Don't rush to attack your attacker,
Leave him to the god;

Report him daily to the god,
(15) Tomorrow being like today,
And you will see what the god does,
When he injures him who Injured you.

Study Notes:

THE PRINCIPLE OF SEX-SUBLIMATION

(19) "I have not committed adultery." **<u>Variant: And homosexuality.</u>**
(27) "I have not lusted or committed fornication." **<u>Variant: or sex with a boy.</u>**

<u>Sage Ptahotep</u>

18. If you want friendship to endure
In the house you enter
As master, brother, or friend,
In whatever place you enter,
Beware of approaching the women.
Unhappy is the place where it is done,
Unwelcome is he who intrudes on them.
A thousand men are turned -away from their good: A short moment is like a dream,
Then death comes for having known them.
Poor advice is "shoot the opponent,"
When one goes to do it the heart rejects it.
He who fails through lust of them,
No affair of his can prosper.

37- If you take to wife a good woman
Who is joyful and known by her town,
If she is fickle and likes the moment,
Do not reject her, let her eat,
The joyful brings happiness.

<u>Sage Ani</u>

Beware of a woman who is a stranger,
One not known in her town;
Don't stare at her when she goes by,
Do not know her carnally.
A deep water whose course is unknown,
Such is a woman away from her husband.
"I am pretty," she tells you daily,
When she has no witnesses;
She is ready to ensnare you,
A great deadly crime when it is heard.

Do not control your wife in her house,
When you know she is efficient;
Don't say to her: "Where is it? Get it!"
When she has put it in the right place.
Let your eye observe in silence,
Then you recognize her skill,
It is joy when your hand is with her,

Study Notes:

There are many who don't know this.
If a man desists from strife at home,
He will not encounter its beginning.
Every man who founds a household
Should hold back the hasty heart.
Do not go after a woman,
Let her not steal your heart.

Chapter 137A of the *Book of Coming Forth By Day* states:

> *And behold, these things shall be performed by one who is clean, and is ceremonially pure, a man who hath eaten neither meat nor fish, and who hath not had intercourse with women* (applies to female initiates not having intercourse with men as well).

ANCIENT EGYPTIAN PROVERBS ON THE RELATIONSHIP BETWEEN WOMAN AND MAN

"When thou find sensibility of heart, joined with softness of manners, an accomplished mind, with a form agreeable to thy fancy, take her home to thy house; she is worthy to be thy friend, thy companion in life, the wife of thy bosom."

"Remember thou art man's reasonable companion, not the slave of his passion; the end of thy being is not merely to gratify his loose desire, but to assist him in the toils of life, to soothe him with thy tenderness, and recompense his care and like treatment with soft endearments."

"When you prosper and establish your home, love your wife with ardor. Then fill her belly and clothe her back. Caress her. Give her ointments to soothe her body. Fulfill her wishes for as long as you live. She is a fertile field for her husband. Do not be brutal. Good manners will influence her better than force. Do not contend with her in the courts. Keep her from the need to resort to outside powers. Her eye is her storm when she gazes. It is by such treatment that she will be compelled to stay in your house."

Study Notes:

THE SCALES OF MAAT AND THE PSYCHOSPIRITUAL ENERGY CENTERS

Scene from the Greenfield Papyrus.

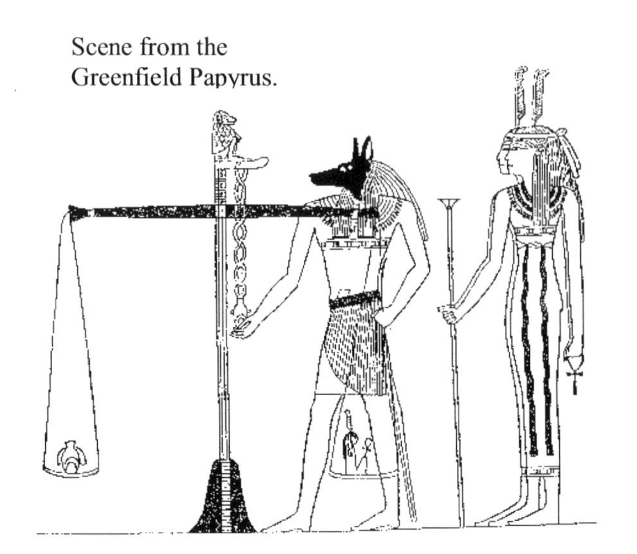

Book of Coming Forth By Day (Papyrus) of Kenna

Maat philosophy ancompases the highly mystical teachings related to the psychospiritual energy centers. This is the Serpent Power or Arat. In India this system of spiritual philosophy is known as Kundalini Yoga. The Life Force energy is latent in the spiritual body of every human being. As it is awakened, by following the teachings of Maat, it leads a person to awaken in spiritual consciousness. Maat can be seen (above) presiding over the scale. It is determining the level of righteousness of the heart of the person in question but also the spiritual level of evolution. There are seven spiritual centers which operate in the subtle body of a human being. They are represented by seven spheres or chain links. Each represents a psychospiritual principle which must be mastered in order to evolve spiritually. Those who do not evolve are devouwered by the Ammit monster. The first center represents fear and the basic necessities of life (Eating and elimination). The second center represents creativity and sexuality. The third center represents ego control over others (negative will power) and personal energy. The fourth center represents selfless love. The fifth center relresents self-control and positive will power. Ther sixth center represents the Eye of Heru, intuitional vision of the spirit world as well as the phenominal world. The seventh center represents transcendental vision and becoming one with God. Evolution implies getting beyond the first three lower centers. The masses of people are entangled with the world due to their egoism, desires and worldly concerns. This is what the lower three centers represents. The upper four centers represent the process of spiritual evolution and selfdiscovery. See the book “The Serpent Power” by Dr. Muata Ashby.

Study Notes:

The energy centers of the subtle body are likened to a tree which the aspirant climbs through personality integration, which leads him/her to intuitional realization of the transcendental self. In the process of creation, the creative energy manifests in the form of six planes of consciousness. This is the realm of phenomenal reality including physical, astral and mental existence. Most people function on the level of the first three energy-consciousness levels. The goal of this Yoga (Serpent Power) is to unite the six phenomenal consciousness centers with the seventh or transcendental realm of consciousness, the Absolute. This Absolute is what various religions refer to by different names such as the Kingdom of Heaven, Osiris, Krishna, Brahman, the Tao, God, Higher Self, Goddess, Christ, Buddha, etc.

Kundalini energy, known as Prana, chi, and Ra-Sekhem, flows throughout thousands of *Nadis* or energy channels. If any of the energy channels are blocked or over-sensitized, a dis-balance can arise, causing illness in the mind and physical body. There are three most important channels through which the Serpent Power flows. In India these are known as: *Sushumna, Ida and Pingala* -These are represented by the Egyptian Caduceus of Djehuti which is composed of a staff which has two serpents wrapped around it. During the ceremonies connected to the mysteries of the Uraeus serpent Goddess *Uatchet* (Udjat), the priest addresses the initiate:

> *The Goddess Uatchet cometh unto thee in the form of the living Uraeus* (𓆗Arat), *to anoint thy head with their flames. She riseth up on the left side of thy head, and she shineth from the right side of thy temples without speech; they,(𓆗𓆗Arati), rise up on thy head during each and every hour of the day, even as they do for their father Ra, and through them the terror which thou inspirest in the holy spirits is increased, and because Uatchet and Nekhebet rise up on thy head, and because thy brow becometh the portion of thy head whereon they establish themselves, even as they do upon the brow of Ra, and because they never leave thee, awe of thee striketh into the souls which are made perfect.*

The preceding scripture from the Ancient Egyptian embalming ceremonies is echoed in the *Book of Coming Forth By Day*. The state of enlightenment is further described in Chapters 83 and 85 where the initiate realizes that the seven Uraeus deities or bodies (immortal parts of the spirit) have been reconstituted:

"The seven Uraeuses are my body... my image is now eternal."

These seven Uraeuses, *Iarut,* are also described as the *"seven souls of Ra"* and *"the seven arms of the balance (Maat)"*

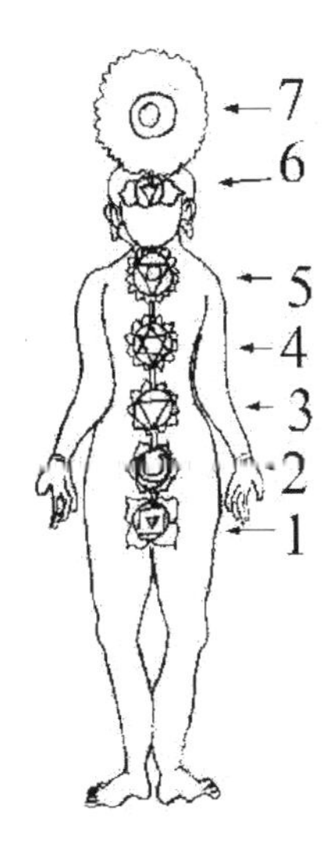

Left: Picture from Indian Kundalini Yoga showing the location of the energy centers.

Right: the God Asar from Ancient Egypt displaying the four upper psycho-spiritual energy centers.

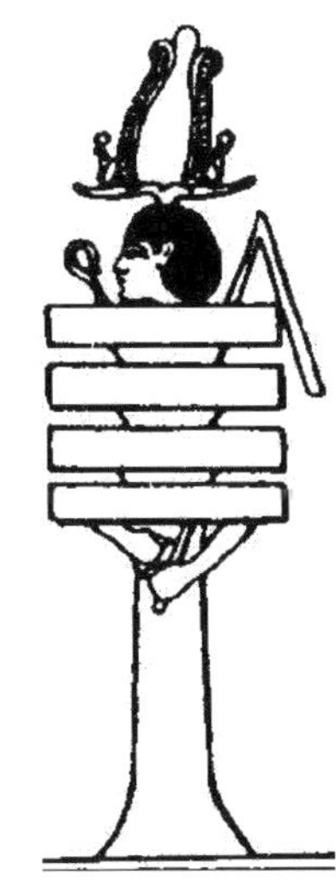

Study Notes:

EVOLUTIONARY MODEL OF MAAT AND THE SERPENT POWER

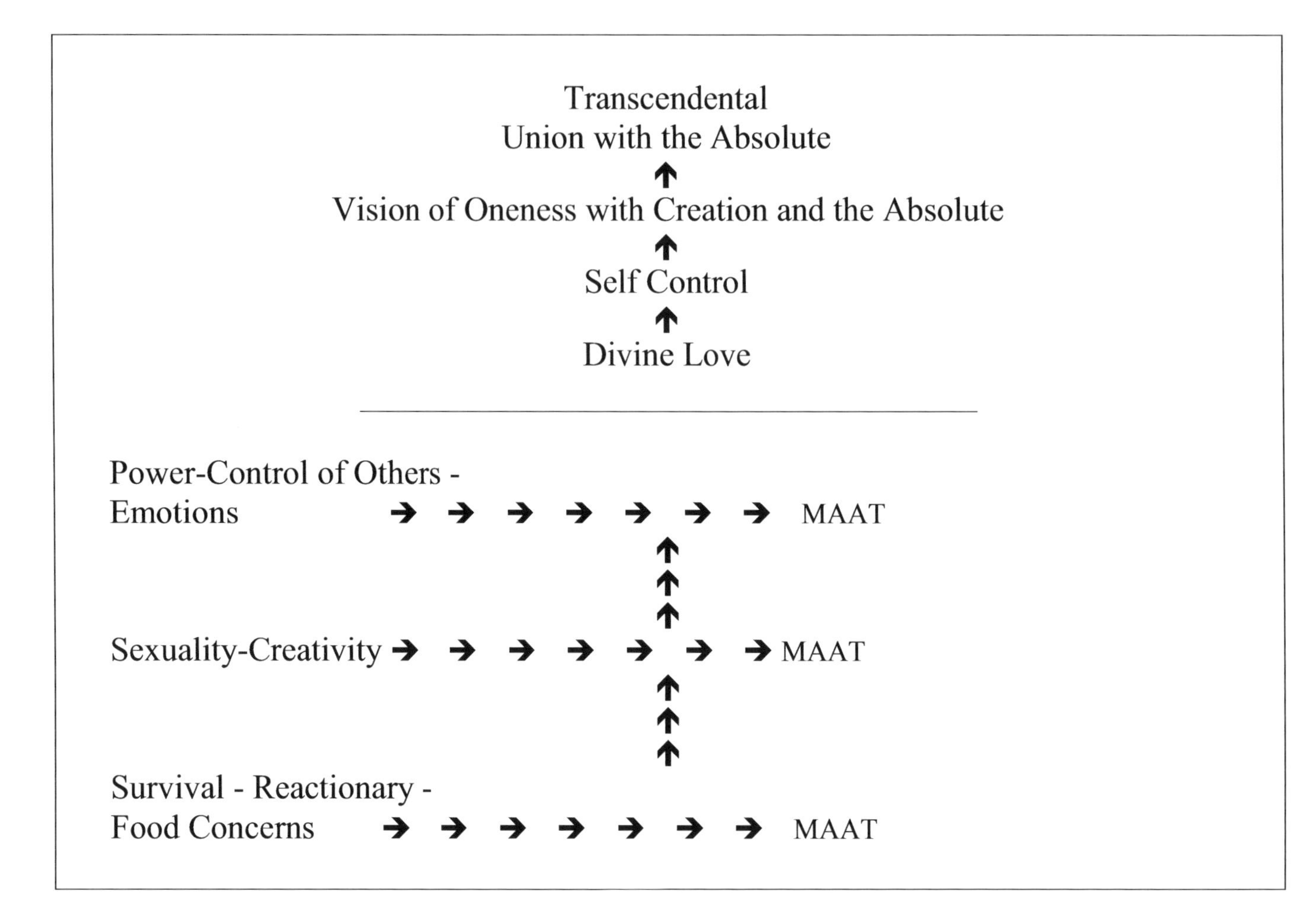

Those who have gained control over the first three psycho-spiritual consciousness centers will be able to discover a new, deeper essence of their own existence as they move beyond "animal" consciousness. Otherwise, they will remain in a horizontal movement through life which will lead to pain, sorrow and disappointments as well as the development of a karmic basis for reincarnation.

Study Notes:

THE SEVEN STEPS OF MAAT

7
Spiritual Enlightenment and Immortality
(Discovery that Maat is All)

6

Outer Harmony (Pace with nature)

Inner Harmony (Fulfillment and Peace)

5

Mental Balance (Equanimity)

4
Expansion of the Heart Through
Selfless Service to Humanity

3
Sublimation of the Ego

2
Self-Control, Sex Sublimation and Non-
Violence (As disciplinary practice)

1
Living In Accordance With What is True
(Right Actions)

Study Notes:

1
Living In Accordance With What is True
(Right Actions)

(7) “I have not acted deceitfully.” Variant: With crookedness.
(24) “I have not stopped my ears against the words of right and wrong (Maat).”
(10) "I have not snatched away food."

2
Self-Control, Sex Sublimation and Non-Violence (As disciplinary practice)

(2) "I have not robbed with violence."
(5) “I have not murdered man or woman.” Variant: Or ordered someone else to commit murder.
(11) “I have not uttered evil words.” Variant: Or allowed myself to become sullen, to sulk or become depressed.
(12) "I have attacked no one."
(30) "I have not acted insolently or with violence."
(19) “I have not committed adultery.” Variant: And homosexuality.
(27) “I have not lusted or committed fornication nor have I lain with others of my same sex.” Variant: or sex with a boy.

3
Sublimation of the Ego

(18) "I have not allowed myself to become angry without cause."
(28) “I have not avenged myself.” Variant: Resentment.
(33) "I have not multiplied my speech overmuch."
(34) “I have not done harm or evil.” Variant: Thought evil.
(39) “I have not behaved with arrogance.” Variant: Boastful.
(40) "I have not been overweeningly proud or sought for distinctions."
(41) “I have never magnified my condition beyond what was fitting or increased my wealth, except with such things as are (justly) mine own possessions by means of Maat.” Variant: I have not disputed over possessions except when they concern my own rightful possessions. Variant: I have not desired more than what is rightfully mine.

Study Notes:

4
Expansion of the Heart Through
Selfless Service to Humanity

(29) "I have not worked grief, I have not abused anyone." Variant: Quarrelsome nature.
(40) "I have not been overwhelmingly proud or sought for distinctions for myself (Selfishness)."

Live upon truth,
Feed upon truth,

Performed the ordinances of men, and the things, which gratify the gods. Propitiate the God by doing his will,
Given bread to the hungry man,
and water to him that was athirst, and apparel to the naked man, and a ferry boat to he who has no boat...
—From the Ancient Egyptian Papyrus of Nu

5
Mental Balance (Equanimity)

(14) "I have not eaten my heart" (overcome with anguish and distraught). Variant: Committed perjury.
(16) "I have not been an eavesdropper or pried into matters to make mischief." Variant: Spy.
(18) "I have not allowed myself to become angry without cause." Variant: Not adopted a quarrelsome nature.
(31) "I have not judged hastily." Variant: or been impatient.
(39) "I have not behaved with arrogance." Variant: Boastful.

6
Outer Harmony & Inner Harmony
(Peace with nature - Fulfillment-Contentment and Peace)

> "In all thy undertaking, let a reasonable assurance animate thy endeavors; if thou despair of success, thou shalt not succeed.

(4) "I have not committed theft." Variant: Coveted.
(I 5) "I have not laid waste the ploughed lands."
(36) "I have never befouled the water."
(25) "I have not stirred up strife (disturbance)." "I have not caused terror." "I have not struck fear into any man."
(26) "I have not caused any one to weep."
(16) "I have not been an eavesdropper or pried into matters to make mischief." Variant: Spy.

Study Notes:

THE PERFECTION OF MAAT: SPIRITUAL ENLIGHTENMENT AND IMMORTALITY

MOVEMENT INTO THE SIXTH ENERGY CENTER

CHAPTER 125-A PLATE 30

ENTERING INTO THE HALL OF MAATI TO PRAISE ASAR KHENTI-AMENTI.

The Asar the scribe Ani, whose word is truth, saith:- I have come unto thee. I have drawn nigh to behold thy beauties (thy beneficent goodness). My hands are [extended] in adoration of thy name of "Maat." I have come. I have drawn nigh unto [the place where] the cedar-tree existeth not, where the acacia tree doth not put forth shoots, and where the ground produceth neither grass nor herbs. Now I have entered into the habitation which is hidden, and I hold converse with Set. My protector advanced to me, covered was his face.... on the hidden things. He entered into the house of Asar, he saw the hidden things which were therein. The Tchatchau Chiefs of the Pylons were in the form of Spirits. The god Anpu spoke unto those about him with the words of a man who cometh from Ta-mera, saying, "He knoweth our roads and our towns. I am reconciled unto him. When I smell his odor it is even as the odor of one of you." And I say unto him: I the Asar Ani, whose word is truth, in peace, whose word is truth, have come. I have drawn nigh to behold the Great Gods. I would live upon the propitiatory offerings [made] to their Doubles. I would live on the borders [of the territory of] the Soul, the Lord of Tetu. He shall make me to come forth in the form of a Benu bird, and to hold converse [with him.] I have been in the stream [to purify myself]. I have made offerings of incense. I betook myself to the Acacia Tree of the [divine] Children. I lived in Abu in the House of the goddess Satet. I made to sink in the water the boat of the enemies. I sailed over the lake [in the temple] in the Neshmet Boat. I have looked upon the Sahu of Kamur. I have been in Tetu. I have held my peace. I have made the god to be master of his legs. I have been in the House of Teptuf. I have seen him, that is the Governor of the Hall of the God. I have entered into the House of Asar and I have removed the head-coverings of him that is therein. I have entered into Rasta, and I have seen the Hidden One who is therein. I was hidden, but I found the boundary. I journeyed to Nerutef, and he who was therein covered me with a garment. I have myrrh of women, together with the shenu powder of living folk. Verily he (Asar) told me the things which concerned himself. I said: Let thy weighing of me be even as we desire. And the Majesty of Anpu shall say unto me, "Knowest thou the name of this door, and canst thou tell it?" And the Asar the scribe Ani, whose word is truth, in peace, whose word is truth, shall say, "Khersek-Shu" is the name of this door. And the Majesty of the god Anpu shall say unto me, "Knowest thou the name of the upper leaf, and the name of the lower leaf?" [And the Asar the scribe Ani] shall say: "Neb-Maat-heri-retiu- f" is the name of the upper leaf and "Neb-pehti-thesu-menment" [is the name of the lower leaf. And the Majesty of the god Anpu shall say], "Pass on, for thou hast knowledge, O Asar the scribe, the assessor of the holy offerings of all the gods of Thebes Ani, whose word is truth, the lord of loyal service [to Asar]."

Study Notes:

Chapter 125 RUBRIC: THE MAKING OF THE REPRESENTATION OF WHAT SHALL HAPPEN IN THIS HALL OF MAATI.

This Chapter shall be recited or chanted by the spiritual aspirant when he is cleansed and purified, and is arrayed in linen apparel, and is shod with sandals of white leather, and his eyes are painted with antimony, and his body is anointed with unguent made of myrrh. And he shall present as offerings oxen, and feathered fowl, and incense, and cakes and ale, and garden herbs. And behold, thou shalt draw a representation of this (Hetep Slab) in color upon a new tile molded from earth upon which neither a pig nor any other animal hath trodden. And if this book be done [in writing, the deceased] shall flourish, and his children shall flourish, and [his name] shall never fall into oblivion, and he shall be as one who fills the heart of the king and of his princes. And bread, and cakes, and sweetmeats, and wine, and pieces of flesh shall be given unto him [from among those which are] upon the altar of the Great God. And he shall not be driven back from any door in Amentet, and he shall be led along with the kings of the South and the kings of the North, and he shall be in the company of Osiris, continually and regularly for ever. [And he shall come forth in every form he pleaseth as a living soul for ever, and ever, and ever.]

This Teaching is effective a million times...

Study Notes:

MOVEMENT INTO THE SEVENTH ENERGY CENTER

7
Spiritual Enlightenment and Immortality
(Discovery that Maat is All)

*"Those who live today will die tomorrow, those who die tomorrow will be born again;
Those who live MAAT will not die."*

–Ancient Egyptian Proverb

"No one reaches the beneficent West unless their heart is righteous by doing MAAT. There is no distinction made between the inferior and the superior person; it only matters that one is found faultless when the balances and the two weights stand before the Lord of Eternity. No one is free from the reckoning. Djehuti, a baboon, holds the balances to count each one according to what they have done upon earth."

–Ancient Egyptian Proverb

"Maat is in every place that is yours ....
You rise with Maat; you live with Maat,
You join your limbs to Maat,
You make Maat rest on your head in order that She may take Her seat on your forehead.
You become young again in the sight of your daughter Maat, you live from the perfume of Her dew.
Maat is worn like an amulet at your throat;
She rests on your chest,
the Divine Entities reward you with Maat, for they know Her wisdom....
Your right eye is Maat,
Your left eye is Maat,
Your flesh,
Your members are Maat....
Your food is Maat,
Your drink is Maat,
The breaths of your nose are Maat....
You exist because Maat exists and vice versa.'

–Berlin Papyrus

*I am pure. I am pure. I am Pure.
I have washed my front parts with the waters of libations, I have cleansed my hinder parts with drugs, which make wholly clean, and my inward parts have been washed in the liquor of Maat.*

—The Scribe Nu

Study Notes:

HOW TO PRACTICE MAAT:

Practicing the philosophy of MAAT means a gradual "becoming" process. "Becoming" implies that one transforms oneself through one's actions from an egoistic personality into a source of universal peace and caring for all humanity. Through your study of this volume you will discover that Maat Philosophy involves the following practices:

-studying the wisdom teachings,
-selfless service,
-wisdom in action (Karma Yoga),
-dedication of all actions to the Divine as a form of Devotional Love.

These dynamic elements are to be practiced in everyday life. Their practice serves to purify the heart (conscious, subconscious and unconscious levels of mind) so as to render it subtle and clear of complexes and agitation. When this purification process reaches a high degree of perfection, the human soul unites with the Universal Soul or God, who is the source of Supreme Peace - HETEP.

HOW TO STUDY THE WISDOM TEACHINGS:

There is a specific technique which is prescribed by the scriptures themselves for studying the teachings, proverbs and aphorisms of mystical wisdom. The method is as follows:

The spiritual aspirant should read the desired text thoroughly, taking note of any particular teachings which resonates with him or her.

The aspirant should make a habit of collecting those teachings and reading them over frequently. The scriptures should be read and re-read because the subtle levels of the teachings will be increasingly understood the more the teachings are reviewed.

One useful exercise is to choose some of the most special teachings you would like to focus on and place them in large type or as posters in your living areas so as to be visible to remind you of the teaching.

The aspirant should discuss those teachings with others of like mind when possible because this will help to promote greater understanding and act as an active spiritual practice in which the teachings are kept at the forefront of the mind. In this way, the teachings can become an integral part of everyday life and not reserved for a particular time of day or of the week.

The study of the wisdom teachings should be a continuous process in which the teachings become the predominant factor of life rather than the useless and oftentimes negative and illusory thoughts of those who are ignorant of spiritual truths. This spiritual discipline should be observed until Enlightenment is attained.

STUDY NOTES:

ANCIENT EGYPTIAN WISDOM AND THE TEACHINGS OF THE BIBLE

THE ANCIENT EGYPTIAN ORIGINS OF THE WISDOM TEACHINGS OF THE BIBLE

THE TEN COMMANDMENTS AND THE PRECEPTS OF MAAT

The similarity between the Ten Commandments, along with the other rules and regulations given to Moses by God in the other books of the Old Testament and the 42 Laws of Maat from Ancient Egypt further unveils the close association between Jewish and Ancient Egyptian religious morality. A simple comparison of the following biblical scriptures to the more Ancient Egyptian ones uncovers the ancient pre-Christian origins of the norms of ethical conduct. A life of ethical conduct was and is the first essential step in the practice of spirituality. The reader will also notice that one of the main teachings of Jesus, to love thy neighbor (non-violence), already existed in both the Ancient Egyptian scriptures and in the Old Testament, long before the birth of Jesus. The following list of commandments comes from the Old Testament of the Bible, the book of Exodus. The subsequent text comes from the Book of Leviticus, which contains segments of the additional laws given to Moses by God. You may directly compare these to the 42 Laws or Precepts of Maat by looking up the specific law to which it corresponds. Simply look for a number in parenthesis, ( ), after the Bible text. This is the number of the specific Precept of Maat from the list which follows after the text of Leviticus.

The Ten Commandments of The Judeo-Christian Tradition

Exodus 20 3:17

1. Thou shalt have no other Gods before me. (Neberdjer and Pa-Neter philosophy of Ancient Egypt)
2. Thou shalt not make to thee any graven image. (Neteru philosophy of Ancient Egypt)
3. Thou shalt not take the name of the Lord thy God in vain (38)
4. Remember the Sabbath day, to keep it holy. (21)
5. Honor thy father and thy mother. (Contained in the wisdom texts of Ancient Egypt.)
6. Thou shalt not kill. (The ancient Hebrew: Thou shall not commit murder.) (5)
7. Thou shalt not commit adultery. (19)
8. Thou shalt not steal. (4), (8)
9. Thou shalt not bear false witness against thy neighbor. (17)
10. Thou shalt not covet thy neighbors house, thou shalt not covet thy neighbors wife, nor his male servant, nor his female servant, nor his ox, nor his donkey, nor any thing that [is] thy neighbors. (41)

Leviticus 18

22 Thou shalt not lie with mankind, as with womankind: it [is] abomination. (27)

26 Ye shall therefore keep my statutes and my judgments, and shall not commit [any] of these abominations; [neither] any of your own nation, nor any stranger that sojourneth among you...(22)

Leviticus 19

11. Ye shall not steal (2), (4), neither deal falsely (7), neither lie (9) one to another.

12 And ye shall not swear by my name falsely, neither shalt thou profane the name of thy God: I [am] the Lord. (32), (42)

13 Thou shalt not defraud thy neighbor, neither rob [him]: (4), (41)

15 Ye shall do no unrighteousness in judgment: thou shalt not respect the person of the poor, nor honor the person of the mighty: [but] in righteousness shalt thou judge thy neighbor. (31)

17 Thou shalt not hate thy brother in thy heart...(20), (42)

18 Thou shalt not avenge, nor bear any grudge against the children of thy people, but thou shalt love thy neighbor as thyself: I [am] the Lord. (28)

30. Ye shall keep my Sabbaths, and reverence my sanctuary: I [am] the Lord. (8), (21)

33 And if a stranger shall sojourn with thee in your land, ye shall not oppress him. {vex: or, oppress}

34 [But] the stranger that dwelleth with you shall be to you as one born among you, and thou shalt love him as thyself; for ye were strangers in the land of Egypt: I [am] the Lord your God. (29)

35 Ye shall do no unrighteousness in judgment, in length, in weight, or in volume. (6)

Leviticus 20
13 If a man also shall lie with mankind, as he lieth with a woman, both of them have committed an abomination: they shall surely be put to death; their blood [shall be] upon them. (27)

Leviticus 22
32 Neither shall ye profane my holy name; but I will be hallowed among the children of Israel: I [am] the Lord who hallow you... (38)

The first two commandments (1. Thou shalt have no other Gods before me and 2. Thou shalt not make to thee any graven image) are an attempt to separate the new Jewish religion from the religion of Ancient Egypt. Since the Ancient Egyptian religion was seen as polytheistic by those who did not have higher understanding, it was assumed to be a confusing hodgepodge of differing idols. However, a deeper study of Ancient Egyptian religion reveals that at no time was polytheism promoted or espoused. The practice of making graven images of God was also never practiced in Ancient Egypt. What was engraved on walls and inscriptions were the wisdom teachings related to God as they manifest in Creation. This is referred to as the Medu Neter (Nedjer). The Medu Neter extols the mythology related to the neteru. Neteru are the cosmic forces which constitute and sustain Creation and human existence. These were symbolized as gods and goddesses. The idea of a nameless, formless, indefinable, inscrutable supreme being occurs first in Ancient Egypt. The name for this concept was a reference to the "Divinity of Light" and later the terms "Neberdjer" or Pa-Neter were used. ***Pa-Neter*** means "The Supreme Being" (see precept #38 and 42 below) as opposed to ***neteru***, which means the emanations from the Supreme Being. It is comparable to the "I am that I am" or "Yahweh" (Jehovah) of the Hebrews and "Brahman" of the Hindus. Thus, it is clear that the ten commandments are an attempt at a reinterpretation of the wisdom teachings of Ancient Egypt, albeit with some areas of incomplete understanding of Ancient Egyptian religious philosophy.

The teachings related to honoring one's parents were a very important ethical and social aspect of Ancient Egyptian life. Therefore, we find precepts related to this issue in the Ancient Egyptian Wisdom texts, the writings upon which the forty-two precepts of Maat are based.

From the Instructions of Sage Ani:

> Libate for your father and mother,
> Who are resting in the valley (deceased)…
>
> Double the food your mother gave you,
> Support her as she supported you…

The 42 Laws or Precepts of Maat were the basis of Ancient Egyptian philosophy at least 2,000 years before Christianity. They were declarations which the initiate was to utter upon being judged by the gods and goddesses as being righteous or not. The judgement is symbolized by the scales of balance where the heart[18] of an individual is weighed against the feather of Maat. Maat is the goddess of truth. There is a god or goddess (guardian angel or patron saint in Christian terminology) who presides over each precept of Maat. An individual is judged by how they were able to follow the Precepts. If the heart is light, meaning that they kept the laws, they can answer affirmatively ("I have not done so and so") and thereby discover God. If they cannot answer affirmatively they will experience hellish conditions. Either way an individual's fate is not determined by some God "up" there but by himself or herself, by means of his or her actions while alive. The scales in Ancient Egypt very closely resemble the Christian symbol called *DIIS Manubus* meaning "To the spirit of the blessed."

The following tables show how Ancient Egyptian wisdom was adopted by the early Jews and incorporated into the teachings of the Bible. Beyond this however, it must also be understand that the objective is not just to show the origins of Judaism in Ancient Egypt, but to point to a deeper understanding of those same teachings so that our understanding of the Bible may be more profound and our spiritual practice of Christianity more intense and fruitful. The wisdom teachings provide us with guidelines for how to conduct our daily affairs. This is important because if we do not have harmony in our day to day life, our spiritual practice will be unbalanced. Therefore, the wisdom teachings and their proper practice are the first step in a viable spiritual program for life.

The following charts are a comparison of the teachings of Ancient Egypt with those of civilizations and religions which developed after and were influenced by Shetaut Neter (Ancient Egyptian Religion). They are presented here in this way for

[18] Will be explained further in the next section.

the sake of showing their origins in previous teachings as well as to give a greater depth in understanding them. Many Egyptologists now believe that the early Jews were well aquatinted with the Ancient Egyptian Wisdom Texts, especially the *Instructions of Amenemope*. The *Instructions of Amenemope* is strikingly similar in concept and the form of the literary expression with the Bible book of Proverbs.

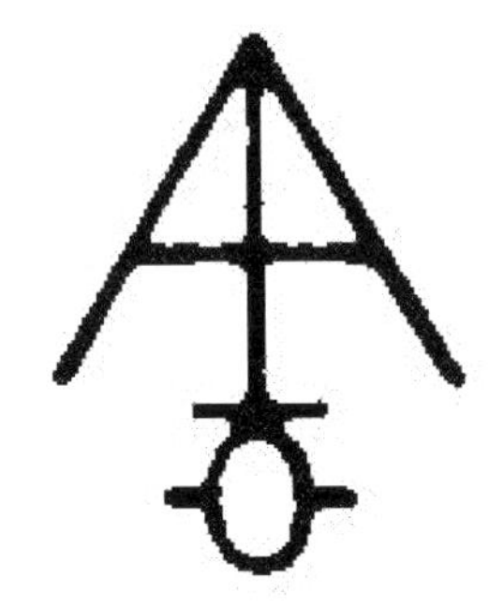

Far left: The Ancient Egyptian Hieroglyph symbolizing the Judgement of the Heart on the Scales of Truth.
Right: The Christian Symbol: DIIS Manubus: To the spirit of the blessed.

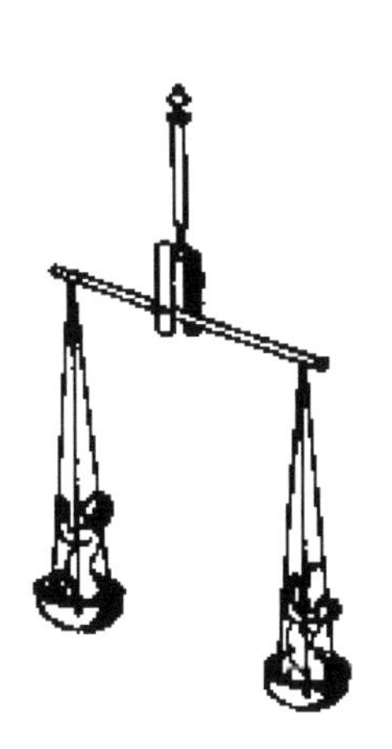

Far left: The Ancient Egyptian Judgement Scales of Maat.

Left: The scales of Christian mythology. In Christian art, the archangel Michael is frequently portrayed holding a pair of scales. One of his responsibilities is to weigh the soul of the dead.[C-1]

THE TEN COMMANDMENTS AND THEIR ORIGINS IN ANCIENT EGYPTIAN WISDOM

The Ten Commandments and the Teachings of Maat:

TEN COMMANDMENTS	TEACHINGS OF MAAT (Ancient Egypt)
Exodus 20 3:17 1. Thou shalt have no other Gods before me.	(30) "One should revere The God (Supreme Being)"*
2. Thou shalt not make to thee any graven image.	(42) "I have never thought evil or slighted the God in my native town." (64) There is no perfection before The God**
3 Thou shalt not take the name of the Lord thy God in vain.	(38) "I have not cursed the God."
4 Remember the Sabbath day, to keep it holy.	(21) "I have not violated sacred times and seasons. "
5. Honor thy father and thy mother.	Thou shalt never forget what thy mother has done for thee, she beareth thee and nourished thee in all manner of ways.***
6. Thou shalt not kill.	(5) "I have not murdered man or woman."'
7. Thou shalt not commit adultery.	(19) "I have not committed adultery."
8. Thou shalt not steal.	(4) "I have not committed theft."
9. Thou shalt not bear false witness against thy neighbor.	(17) "I have not spoken against anyone."
10. Thou shalt not covet thy neighbor's house, thou shalt not covet thy neighbors wife, or his male servant, or his female servant, or his ox., or his donkey, or any thing that is of thy neighbors.	(41) "I have never magnified my condition beyond what was fitting or increased my wealth, except with such things as are a justly mine own possessions." *The Instructions of Merikara (c. 2,135-2,040 B.C.E.) **The Instructions of Amenemope (c. 1,500-1,200 B.C.E) ***Egyptian Proverbs

THE TEACHINGS OF THE BIBLE AND THE TEACHINGS OF SAGE AMENEMOPE

THE TEACHINGS OF THE BIBLE	THE TEACHINGS OF AMENEMOPE (Ancient Egypt)
PROVERBS XXII. 17-XXIII. 14; The "teachings of King Solomon" 0 Israel	
1. Incline thine ear, and hear my words, And apply thine heart to apprehend; For it is pleasant if thou keep them in thy belly,	1. Give thine ear and hear what I say, And apply thine heart to apprehend; It is good for thee to place them in thine heart,
1a. That they may be fixed like a peg upon thy lips.	1a. Let them rest in the casket of thy belly. That they rally act as a peg upon thy tongue.
2. Have I not written for thee thirty sayings of counsels and knowledge! That thou mayest make known truth to him that speaketh.	2. Consider these thirty chapters; they delight, they instruct. Know how to answer one who speaks, To reply to one who sends a message. So as to direct him on the paths of life…
3. Rob not the poor for he is poor, neither oppress the lowly in the gate.	3. Beware of robbing the poor, and of oppressing the afflicted.
4. Associate not with a passionate man, nor go with a wrathful man, lest thou learn his ways and get a snare to thy soul.	4. Associate not with a passionate man, nor approach him for conversations: Leap not to cleave to such a one, that the terror carry thee not away
5. A man who is skillful in his business shall stand before kings.	5. A scribe who is skillful in his business findeth himself worthy to be a courtier.

THE TEACHINGS OF THE BIBLE AND THE TEACHINGS OF SAGE PTAHOTEP

The Teachings of the Bible	**The Teachings of Ptahotep** (Ancient Egypt c. 2,300-2,150 B.C.E.)
PROVERBS 3:7; " Be not wise in thy own eyes: fear the LORD, and depart from evil."	1) "Don't be proud of your knowledge"
PROVERBS: 27.1; "Boast not thyself of tomorrow; for thou knowest not what a day may bring forth."	2) "One plans the morrow but knows not what will be."
PROVERBS 25:9; "Debate thy cause with thy neighbor himself; and discover not a secret to another."	3) "If you probe the character of a friend, don't inquire, but approach him, deal with him alone....."
PROVERBS 25:13; "As the cold snow in the time of harvest, so is a faithful messenger to them that send him: for he refresheth the soul of his masters."	4) "If you are a man of trust, sent by one great man to another, adhere to the nature of him who sent you, give his message as he said it."
PROVERBS 9:9; "Give instruction to a wise man, and he will be yet wiser: teach a just man, and he will increase in learning."	5) "Teach the great what is useful to him."
PSALM 78:5; "For he established a testimony in Jacob, and appointed a law in Israel, which he commanded our fathers, that they should make them known to their children: 6; That the generation to come might know them, even the children which should be born; who should arise and declare them to their children:"	6) "If every word is carried on, they will not perish in the land."
ECCLESIASTES 6:2; "A man to whom God hath given riches, wealth, and honor, so that he wanteth nothing for his soul of all that he desireth, yet God giveth him not power to eat thereof, but a stranger eateth it: this is vanity, and it is an evil disease."	7) "Guard against the vice of greed: a grievous sickness without cure. There is no treatment for it."
ECCLESIASTES 9:17; "The words of wise men are heard in quiet more than the cry of him that ruleth among fools."	8) "If you are a man of worth who sits in his master's council, concentrate on excellence, your silence is better than chatter... gain respect through knowledge ... "
PROVERBS 18:21; "Death and life are in the power of the tongue: and they that love it shall eat the fruit thereof."	9) "The wise is known by his wisdom, the great by his good actions; his heart matches his tongue..."
PROVERBS 23:1; "When thou sittest to eat with a ruler, consider diligently what is before thee:"	10) "If you are one among guests at the table of one greater than you, take what he gives as it is set before you."

The Commandments of Jesus	Teachings of Ancient Egypt
Mark 12 28. And one of the scribes came, and having heard them reasoning together, and perceiving that he had answered them well, asked him, Which is the first commandment of all?	
29 And Jesus answered him, The first of all the commandments [is], Hear, O Israel; The Lord our God is one Lord:	4. His unity is Absolute. Amun (God) is One, One [without a second].†
30 And thou shalt love the Lord thy God with all thy heart, and with all thy soul, and with all thy mind, and with all thy strength: this [is] the first commandment.	46. Thy beauties take possession of and carry away all hearts [minds], and love for Thee make all arms to relax, Thy beautiful form make the hands to tremble, and all hearts [minds] melt at the sight of Thee. †
*In the First Letter of John in the Bible it is stated that God is love: 1 John 4:8 8 He that loveth not knoweth not God; for God is love. 1 John 4:16 16 And we have known and believed the love that God hath to us. God is love; and he that dwelleth in love dwelleth in God, and God in him.	In Ancient Egypt love of God was so important that God was referred to as: "Beloved one or love itself God- *Merr*"[132] **(i.e. God is Love)**
31 And the second [is] like, [namely] this, Thou shalt love thy neighbor as thyself. There is no other commandment greater than these.	(30) Set your goodness before people, Then you are greeted by all; One welcomes the what is good, Spits upon what is bad. (31) Guard your tongue from harmful speech, Then others will love you. You will find your place in the Sanctuary, the House of God, Be kind to the poor. Get thee a seat in the sanctuary. Be strong to do the commandment of God. You will share in the offerings of your lord. ‡
<u>Jesus on prayer</u> Matthew 6:6 But thou, when thou prayest, enter into thy closet, and when thou hast shut thy door, pray to thy Father who is in secret; and thy Father who seeth in secret shall reward thee openly.	**<u>Teachings of Sage Ani on prayer</u>** Do not raise your voice in the House of God, He abhors shouting; (too much talking) Pray by yourself with a loving heart, Whose every word is in secret. He will grant your needs, He will hear your words, He will accept your offerings. † Ancient Egyptian Hymns of Amun. (c. 2,500-1,500 B.C.E.) ‡ Ancient Egyptian Teachings of Sage Amenemope.

INDEX

⸸SEMA INSTITUTE OF YOGA ⸸

KEMETIC PHILOSOPHY AND
GNOSTIC CHRISTIAN STUDIES

Sema or Smai (⸸) is the Ancient Egyptian word and symbol meaning *union* of the Higher and Lower Self which leads to spiritual enlightenment in a human being. The Sema Institute is dedicated to the propagation of the universal teachings of spiritual evolution. It is a non-denominational, non-profit organization which recognizes the unifying principles in all spiritual and religious systems of evolution throughout the world. Our primary goals are to provide the wisdom of ancient spiritual teachings in books, courses and other forms of communication. Secondly, to provide expert instruction and training in the various yogic disciplines including Ancient Egyptian Philosophy, Christian Gnosticism, Indian Philosophy and modern science. Thirdly, to promote world peace and Universal Love.

Reginald Muata Ashby D.D., P.C., Y.U.

Reginald Muata Ashby holds a Doctor of Philosophy Degree in Religion and a Doctor of Divinity Degree in Holistic Healing. He is also a Pastoral Counselor and Teacher of Yoga Philosophy and Discipline. Dr. Ashby is an adjunct faculty member of the American Institute of Holistic Theology and an Adjunct Professor of Ancient Egyptian studies at Florida International University. Dr. Ashby is a certification as a PREP Relationship Counselor. Dr. Ashby has been an independent researcher and practitioner of Egyptian, Indian and Chinese Yoga and psychology as well as Christian Mysticism. Dr. Ashby has engaged in Postgraduate research in advanced Jnana, Bhakti and Kundalini Yogas at the Yoga Research Foundation. He has extensively studied mystical religious traditions from around the world and is an accomplished lecturer, artist and author of over 20 books on yoga and spiritual philosophy. He is the originator of the Egyptian Yoga concept. He is an Ordained Minister and Spiritual Counselor and also the founder the Sheti Association, a membership group for the study and practice of Egyptian Yoga as well as the Sema Institute, a non-profit organization dedicated to spreading the wisdom of Yoga and the Ancient Egyptian mystical philosophy and universal spiritual traditions. Dr. Ashby conducts seminars, workshops and presentations nationally.

Other Books From C M Books

P.O.Box 570459
Miami, Florida, 33257
(305) 378-6253 Fax: (305) 378-6253

This book is part of a series on the study and practice of Ancient Egyptian Yoga and Mystical Spirituality based on the writings of Dr. Muata Abhaya Ashby. They are also part of the Egyptian Yoga Course provided by the Sema Institute of Yoga. Below you will find a listing of the other books in this series. For more information send for the Egyptian Yoga Book-Audio-Video Catalog or the Egyptian Yoga Course Catalog.

Now you can study the teachings of Egyptian and Indian Yoga wisdom and Spirituality with the Egyptian Yoga Mystical Spirituality Series. The Egyptian Yoga Series takes you through the Initiation process and lead you to understand the mysteries of the soul and the Divine and to attain the highest goal of life: ENLIGHTENMENT. The ***Egyptian Yoga Series***, takes you on an in depth study of Ancient Egyptian mythology and their inner mystical meaning. Each Book is prepared for the serious student of the mystical sciences and provides a study of the teachings along with exercises, assignments and projects to make the teachings understood and effective in real life. The Series is part of the Egyptian Yoga course but may be purchased even if you are not taking the course. The series is ideal for study groups.

Prices subject to change.

1. EGYPTIAN YOGA: THE PHILOSOPHY OF ENLIGHTENMENT An original, fully illustrated work, including hieroglyphs, detailing the meaning of the Egyptian mysteries, tantric yoga, psycho-spiritual and physical exercises. Egyptian Yoga is a guide to the practice of the highest spiritual philosophy which leads to absolute freedom from human misery and to immortality. It is well known by scholars that Egyptian philosophy is the basis of Western and Middle Eastern religious philosophies such as *Christianity, Islam*, *Judaism,* the *Kabala*, and Greek philosophy, but what about Indian philosophy, Yoga and Taoism? What were the original teachings? How can they be practiced today? What is the source of pain and suffering in the world and what is the solution? Discover the deepest mysteries of the mind and universe within and outside of your self. 8.5" X 11" ISBN: 1-884564-01-1 Soft $19.95

2. EGYPTIAN YOGA II: The Supreme Wisdom of Enlightenment by Dr. Muata Ashby ISBN 1-884564-39-9 $23.95 U.S. In this long awaited sequel to *Egyptian Yoga: The Philosophy of Enlightenment* you will take a fascinating and enlightening journey back in time and discover the teachings which constituted the epitome of Ancient Egyptian spiritual wisdom. What are the disciplines which lead to the fulfillment of all desires? Delve into the three states of consciousness (waking, dream and deep sleep) and the fourth state which transcends them all, Neberdjer, "The Absolute." These teachings of the city of Waset (Thebes) were the crowning achievement of the Sages of Ancient Egypt. They establish the standard mystical keys for understanding the profound mystical symbolism of the Triad of human consciousness.

3. THE KEMETIC DIET: GUIDE TO HEALTH, DIET AND FASTING Health issues have always been important to human beings since the beginning of time. The earliest records of history show that the art of healing was held in high esteem since the time of Ancient Egypt. In the early 20th century, medical doctors had almost attained the status of sainthood by the promotion of the idea that they alone were "scientists" while other healing modalities and traditional healers who did not follow the "scientific method' were nothing but superstitious, ignorant charlatans who at best would take the money of their clients and at worst kill them with the unscientific "snake oils" and "irrational theories". In the late 20th century, the failure of the modern medical establishment's ability to lead the general public to good health, promoted the move by many in society towards "alternative medicine". Alternative medicine disciplines are those healing modalities which do not adhere to the philosophy of allopathic medicine. Allopathic medicine is what medical doctors practice by an large. It is the theory that disease is caused by agencies outside the body such as bacteria, viruses or physical means which affect the body. These can therefore be treated by medicines and therapies The natural healing method began in the absence of extensive technologies with the idea that all the answers for health may be found in nature or rather, the deviation from nature. Therefore, the health of the body can be restored by correcting the aberration and thereby restoring balance. This is the area that will be covered in this volume. Allopathic techniques have their place in the art of healing. However, we should not forget that the body is a grand achievement of the spirit and built into it is the capacity to maintain itself and heal itself. Ashby, Muata ISBN: 1-884564-49-6 $28.95

4. INITIATION INTO EGYPTIAN YOGA Shedy: Spiritual discipline or program, to go deeply into the mysteries, to study the mystery teachings and literature profoundly, to penetrate the mysteries. You will learn about the mysteries

of initiation into the teachings and practice of Yoga and how to become an Initiate of the mystical sciences. This insightful manual is the first in a series which introduces you to the goals of daily spiritual and yoga practices: Meditation, Diet, Words of Power and the ancient wisdom teachings. 8.5" X 11" ISBN 1-884564-02-X Soft Cover $24.95 U.S.

5. *THE AFRICAN ORIGINS OF CIVILIZATION, MYSTICAL RELIGION AND YOGA PHILOSOPHY* HARD COVER EDITION ISBN: 1-884564-50-X $80.00 U.S. 81/2" X 11" Part 1, Part 2, Part 3 in one volume 683 Pages Hard Cover First Edition Three volumes in one. Over the past several years I have been asked to put together in one volume the most important evidences showing the correlations and common teachings between Kamitan (Ancient Egyptian) culture and religion and that of India. The questions of the history of Ancient Egypt, and the latest archeological evidences showing civilization and culture in Ancient Egypt and its spread to other countries, has intrigued many scholars as well as mystics over the years. Also, the possibility that Ancient Egyptian Priests and Priestesses migrated to Greece, India and other countries to carry on the traditions of the Ancient Egyptian Mysteries, has been speculated over the years as well. In chapter 1 of the book *Egyptian Yoga The Philosophy of Enlightenment,* 1995, I first introduced the deepest comparison between Ancient Egypt and India that had been brought forth up to that time. Now, in the year 2001 this new book, *THE AFRICAN ORIGINS OF CIVILIZATION, MYSTICAL RELIGION AND YOGA PHILOSOPHY,* more fully explores the motifs, symbols and philosophical correlations between Ancient Egyptian and Indian mysticism and clearly shows not only that Ancient Egypt and India were connected culturally but also spiritually. How does this knowledge help the spiritual aspirant? This discovery has great importance for the Yogis and mystics who follow the philosophy of Ancient Egypt and the mysticism of India. It means that India has a longer history and heritage than was previously understood. It shows that the mysteries of Ancient Egypt were essentially a yoga tradition which did not die but rather developed into the modern day systems of Yoga technology of India. It further shows that African culture developed Yoga Mysticism earlier than any other civilization in history. All of this expands our understanding of the unity of culture and the deep legacy of Yoga, which stretches into the distant past, beyond the Indus Valley civilization, the earliest known high culture in India as well as the Vedic tradition of Aryan culture. Therefore, Yoga culture and mysticism is the oldest known tradition of spiritual development and Indian mysticism is an extension of the Ancient Egyptian mysticism. By understanding the legacy which Ancient Egypt gave to India the mysticism of India is better understood and by comprehending the heritage of Indian Yoga, which is rooted in Ancient Egypt the Mysticism of Ancient Egypt is also better understood. This expanded understanding allows us to prove the underlying kinship of humanity, through the common symbols, motifs and philosophies which are not disparate and confusing teachings but in reality expressions of the same study of truth through metaphysics and mystical realization of Self. (HARD COVER)

6. AFRICAN ORIGINS BOOK 1 PART 1 African Origins of African Civilization, Religion, Yoga Mysticism and Ethics Philosophy-Soft Cover $24.95 ISBN: 1-884564-55-0

7. AFRICAN ORIGINS BOOK 2 PART 2 African Origins of Western Civilization, Religion and Philosophy(Soft) - Soft Cover $24.95 ISBN: 1-884564-56-9

8. EGYPT AND INDIA (AFRICAN ORIGINS BOOK 3 PART 3) African Origins of Eastern Civilization, Religion, Yoga Mysticism and Philosophy-Soft Cover $29.95 (Soft) ISBN: 1-884564-57-7

9. THE MYSTERIES OF ISIS: **The Ancient Egyptian Philosophy of Self-Realization** - There are several paths to discover the Divine and the mysteries of the higher Self. This volume details the mystery teachings of the goddess Aset (Isis) from Ancient Egypt- the path of wisdom. It includes the teachings of her temple and the disciplines that are enjoined for the initiates of the temple of Aset as they were given in ancient times. Also, this book includes the teachings of the main myths of Aset that lead a human being to spiritual enlightenment and immortality. Through the study of ancient myth and the illumination of initiatic understanding the idea of God is expanded from the mythological comprehension to the metaphysical. Then this metaphysical understanding is related to you, the student, so as to begin understanding your true divine nature. ISBN 1-884564-24-0 $22.99

10. EGYPTIAN PROVERBS: TEMT TCHAAS *Temt Tchaas* means: collection of ——Ancient Egyptian Proverbs How to live according to MAAT Philosophy. Beginning Meditation. All proverbs are indexed for easy searches. For the first time in one volume, ——Ancient Egyptian Proverbs, wisdom teachings and meditations, fully illustrated with hieroglyphic text and symbols. EGYPTIAN PROVERBS is a unique collection of knowledge and wisdom which you can put into practice today and transform your life. 5.5"x 8.5" $14.95 U.S ISBN: 1-884564-00-3

11. THE PATH OF DIVINE LOVE The Process of Mystical Transformation and The Path of Divine Love This Volume focuses on the ancient wisdom teachings of "Neter Merri" –the Ancient Egyptian philosophy of Divine Love and how to use them in a scientific process for self-transformation. Love is one of the most powerful human emotions. It is also the source of Divine feeling that unifies God and the individual human being. When love is fragmented and diminished by egoism the Divine connection is lost. The Ancient tradition of Neter Merri leads human beings back to their Divine connection, allowing them to discover their innate glorious self that is actually Divine and immortal. This volume will detail the process of transformation from ordinary consciousness to cosmic consciousness through the integrated practice of the teachings and the path of Devotional Love toward the Divine. 5.5"x 8.5" ISBN 1-884564-11-9 $22.99

12. INTRODUCTION TO MAAT PHILOSOPHY: Spiritual Enlightenment Through the Path of Virtue Known as Karma Yoga in India, the teachings of MAAT for living virtuously and with orderly wisdom are explained and the student is to begin practicing the precepts of Maat in daily life so as to promote the process of purification of the heart in preparation for the judgment of the soul. This judgment will be understood not as an event that will occur at the time of death but as an event that occurs continuously, at every moment in the life of the individual. The student will learn how to become allied with the forces of the Higher Self and to thereby begin cleansing the mind (heart) of impurities so as to attain a higher vision of reality. ISBN 1-884564-20-8 $22.99

13. MEDITATION The Ancient Egyptian Path to Enlightenment Many people do not know about the rich history of meditation practice in Ancient Egypt. This volume outlines the theory of meditation and presents the Ancient Egyptian Hieroglyphic text which give instruction as to the nature of the mind and its three modes of expression. It also presents the texts which give instruction on the practice of meditation for spiritual Enlightenment and unity with the Divine. This volume allows the reader to begin practicing meditation by explaining, in easy to understand terms, the simplest form of meditation and working up to the most advanced form which was practiced in ancient times and which is still practiced by yogis around the world in modern times. ISBN 1-884564-27-7 $24.99

14. THE GLORIOUS LIGHT MEDITATION TECHNIQUE OF ANCIENT EGYPT ISBN: 1-884564-15-1$14.95 (PB) New for the year 2000. This volume is based on the earliest known instruction in history given for the practice of formal meditation. Discovered by Dr. Muata Ashby, it is inscribed on the walls of the Tomb of Seti I in Thebes Egypt. This volume details the philosophy and practice of this unique system of meditation originated in Ancient Egypt and the earliest practice of meditation known in the world which occurred in the most advanced African Culture.

15. THE SERPENT POWER: The Ancient Egyptian Mystical Wisdom of the Inner Life Force. This Volume specifically deals with the latent life Force energy of the universe and in the human body, its control and sublimation. How to develop the Life Force energy of the subtle body. This Volume will introduce the esoteric wisdom of the science of how virtuous living acts in a subtle and mysterious way to cleanse the latent psychic energy conduits and vortices of the spiritual body. ISBN 1-884564-19-4 $22.95

16. EGYPTIAN YOGA MEDITATION IN MOTION Thef Neteru: *The Movement of The Gods and Goddesses* Discover the physical postures and exercises practiced thousands of years ago in Ancient Egypt which are today known as Yoga exercises. This work is based on the pictures and teachings from the Creation story of Ra, The Asarian Resurrection Myth and the carvings and reliefs from various Temples in Ancient Egypt 8.5" X 11" ISBN 1-884564-10-0 Soft Cover $18.99 Exercise video $21.99

17. EGYPTIAN TANTRA YOGA: The Art of Sex Sublimation and Universal Consciousness This Volume will expand on the male and female principles within the human body and in the universe and further detail the sublimation of sexual energy into spiritual energy. The student will study the deities Min and Hathor, Asar and Aset, Geb and Nut and discover the mystical implications for a practical spiritual discipline. This Volume will also focus on the Tantric aspects of Ancient Egyptian and Indian mysticism, the purpose of sex and the mystical teachings of sexual sublimation which lead to self-knowledge and Enlightenment. 5.5"x 8.5" ISBN 1-884564-03-8 $24.95

18. ASARIAN RELIGION: RESURRECTING OSIRIS The path of Mystical Awakening and the Keys to Immortality NEW REVISED AND EXPANDED EDITION! The Ancient Sages created stories based on human and superhuman beings whose struggles, aspirations, needs and desires ultimately lead them to discover their true Self. The myth of Aset, Asar and Heru is no exception in this area. While there is no one source where the entire story may be found, pieces of it are inscribed in various ancient Temples walls, tombs, steles and papyri. For the first time available, the complete myth of Asar, Aset and Heru has been compiled from original Ancient Egyptian, Greek and Coptic Texts. This epic myth has been richly illustrated with reliefs from the Temple of Heru at Edfu, the

AND THE PHILOSOPHY OF RIGHTEOUS ACTION

Temple of Aset at Philae, the Temple of Asar at Abydos, the Temple of Hathor at Denderah and various papyri, inscriptions and reliefs. Discover the myth which inspired the teachings of the *Shetaut Neter* (Egyptian Mystery System - Egyptian Yoga) and the Egyptian Book of Coming Forth By Day. Also, discover the three levels of Ancient Egyptian Religion, how to understand the mysteries of the Duat or Astral World and how to discover the abode of the Supreme in the Amenta, *The Other World* The ancient religion of Asar, Aset and Heru, if properly understood, contains all of the elements necessary to lead the sincere aspirant to attain immortality through inner self-discovery. This volume presents the entire myth and explores the main mystical themes and rituals associated with the myth for understating human existence, creation and the way to achieve spiritual emancipation - *Resurrection.* The Asarian myth is so powerful that it influenced and is still having an effect on the major world religions. Discover the origins and mystical meaning of the Christian Trinity, the Eucharist ritual and the ancient origin of the birthday of Jesus Christ. Soft Cover ISBN: 1-884564-27-5 $24.95

19. THE EGYPTIAN BOOK OF THE DEAD MYSTICISM OF THE PERT EM HERU $26.95 ISBN# 1-884564-28-3 Size: 8½" X 11" I Know myself, I know myself, I am One With God!–From the Pert Em Heru "The Ru Pert em Heru" or "Ancient Egyptian Book of The Dead," or "Book of Coming Forth By Day" as it is more popularly known, has fascinated the world since the successful translation of Ancient Egyptian hieroglyphic scripture over 150 years ago. The astonishing writings in it reveal that the Ancient Egyptians believed in life after death and in an ultimate destiny to discover the Divine. The elegance and aesthetic beauty of the hieroglyphic text itself has inspired many see it as an art form in and of itself. But is there more to it than that? Did the Ancient Egyptian wisdom contain more than just aphorisms and hopes of eternal life beyond death? In this volume Dr. Muata Ashby, the author of over 25 books on Ancient Egyptian Yoga Philosophy has produced a new translation of the original texts which uncovers a mystical teaching underlying the sayings and rituals instituted by the Ancient Egyptian Sages and Saints. "Once the philosophy of Ancient Egypt is understood as a mystical tradition instead of as a religion or primitive mythology, it reveals its secrets which if practiced today will lead anyone to discover the glory of spiritual self-discovery. The Pert em Heru is in every way comparable to the Indian Upanishads or the Tibetan Book of the Dead." Muata Abhaya Ashby

20. ANUNIAN THEOLOGY THE MYSTERIES OF RA The Philosophy of Anu and The Mystical Teachings of The Ancient Egyptian Creation Myth Discover the mystical teachings contained in the Creation Myth and the gods and goddesses who brought creation and human beings into existence. The Creation Myth holds the key to understanding the universe and for attaining spiritual Enlightenment. ISBN: 1-884564-38-0 40 pages $14.95

21. MYSTERIES OF MIND AND MEMPHITE THEOLOGY Mysticism of Ptah, Egyptian Physics and Yoga Metaphysics and the Hidden properties of Matter This Volume will go deeper into the philosophy of God as creation and will explore the concepts of modern science and how they correlate with ancient teachings. This Volume will lay the ground work for the understanding of the philosophy of universal consciousness and the initiatic/yogic insight into who or what is God? ISBN 1-884564-07-0 $21.95

22. THE GODDESS AND THE EGYPTIAN MYSTERIESTHE PATH OF THE GODDESS THE GODDESS PATH The Secret Forms of the Goddess and the Rituals of Resurrection The Supreme Being may be worshipped as father or as mother. *Ushet Rekhat* or *Mother Worship*, is the spiritual process of worshipping the Divine in the form of the Divine Goddess. It celebrates the most important forms of the Goddess including *Nathor, Maat, Aset, Arat, Amentet and Hathor* and explores their mystical meaning as well as the rising of *Sirius,* the star of Aset (Aset) and the new birth of Hor (Heru). The end of the year is a time of reckoning, reflection and engendering a new or renewed positive movement toward attaining spiritual Enlightenment. The Mother Worship devotional meditation ritual, performed on five days during the month of December and on New Year's Eve, is based on the Ushet Rekhit. During the ceremony, the cosmic forces, symbolized by Sirius - and the constellation of Orion ---, are harnessed through the understanding and devotional attitude of the participant. This propitiation draws the light of wisdom and health to all those who share in the ritual, leading to prosperity and wisdom. $14.95 ISBN 1-884564-18-6

23. *THE MYSTICAL JOURNEY FROM JESUS TO CHRIST* $24.95 ISBN# 1-884564-05-4 size: 8½" X 11" Discover the ancient Egyptian origins of Christianity before the Catholic Church and learn the mystical teachings given by Jesus to assist all humanity in becoming Christlike. Discover the secret meaning of the Gospels that were discovered in Egypt. Also discover how and why so many Christian churches came into being. Discover that the Bible still holds the keys to mystical realization even though its original writings were changed by the church. Discover how to practice the original teachings of Christianity which leads to the Kingdom of Heaven.

24. THE STORY OF ASAR, ASET AND HERU: An Ancient Egyptian Legend (For Children) Now for the first time, the most ancient myth of Ancient Egypt comes alive for children. Inspired by the books *The Asarian Resurrection: The Ancient Egyptian Bible* and *The Mystical Teachings of The Asarian Resurrection, The Story of Asar, Aset and Heru* is an easy to understand and thrilling tale which inspired the children of Ancient Egypt to aspire to greatness and righteousness. If you and your child have enjoyed stories like *The Lion King* and *Star Wars you will love The Story of Asar, Aset and Heru.* Also, if you know the story of Jesus and Krishna you will discover than Ancient Egypt had a similar myth and that this myth carries important spiritual teachings for living a fruitful and fulfilling life. This book may be used along with *The Parents Guide To The Asarian Resurrection Myth: How to Teach Yourself and Your Child the Principles of Universal Mystical Religion.* The guide provides some background to the Asarian Resurrection myth and it also gives insight into the mystical teachings contained in it which you may introduce to your child. It is designed for parents who wish to grow spiritually with their children and it serves as an introduction for those who would like to study the Asarian Resurrection Myth in depth and to practice its teachings. 41 pages 8.5" X 11" ISBN: 1-884564-31-3 $12.95

25. THE PARENTS GUIDE TO THE AUSARIAN RESURRECTION MYTH: How to Teach Yourself and Your Child the Principles of Universal Mystical Religion. This insightful manual brings for the timeless wisdom of the ancient through the Ancient Egyptian myth of Asar, Aset and Heru and the mystical teachings contained in it for parents who want to guide their children to understand and practice the teachings of mystical spirituality. This manual may be used with the children's storybook *The Story of Asar, Aset and Heru* by Dr. Muata Abhaya Ashby. 5.5"x 8.5" ISBN: 1-884564-30-5 $14.95

26. HEALING THE CRIMINAL HEART BOOK 1 Introduction to Maat Philosophy, Yoga and Spiritual Redemption Through the Path of Virtue Who is a criminal? Is there such a thing as a criminal heart? What is the source of evil and sinfulness and is there any way to rise above it? Is there redemption for those who have committed sins, even the worst crimes? Ancient Egyptian mystical psychology holds important answers to these questions. Over ten thousand years ago mystical psychologists, the Sages of Ancient Egypt, studied and charted the human mind and spirit and laid out a path which will lead to spiritual redemption, prosperity and Enlightenment. This introductory volume brings forth the teachings of the Asarian Resurrection, the most important myth of Ancient Egypt, with relation to the faults of human existence: anger, hatred, greed, lust, animosity, discontent, ignorance, egoism jealousy, bitterness, and a myriad of psycho-spiritual ailments which keep a human being in a state of negativity and adversity. 5.5"x 8.5" ISBN: 1-884564-17-8 $15.95

27. THEATER & DRAMA OF THE ANCIENT EGYPTIAN MYSTERIES: Featuring the Ancient Egyptian stage play-"The Enlightenment of Hathor' Based on an Ancient Egyptian Drama, The original Theater -Mysticism of the Temple of Hetheru $14.95 By Dr. Muata Ashby

28. GUIDE TO PRINT ON DEMAND: SELF-PUBLISH FOR PROFIT, SPIRITUAL FULFILLMENT AND SERVICE TO HUMANITY Everyone asks us how we produced so many books in such a short time. Here are the secrets to writing and producing books that uplift humanity and how to get them printed for a fraction of the regular cost. Anyone can become an author even if they have limited funds. All that is necessary is the willingness to learn how the printing and book business work and the desire to follow the special instructions given here for preparing your manuscript format. Then you take your work directly to the non-traditional companies who can produce your books for less than the traditional book printer can. ISBN: 1-884564-40-2 $16.95 U. S.

29. Egyptian Mysteries: Vol. 1, Shetaut Neter ISBN: 1-884564-41-0 $19.99 What are the Mysteries? For thousands of years the spiritual tradition of Ancient Egypt, S*hetaut Neter,* "The Egyptian Mysteries," "The Secret Teachings," have fascinated, tantalized and amazed the world. At one time exalted and recognized as the highest culture of the world, by Africans, Europeans, Asiatics, Hindus, Buddhists and other cultures of the ancient world, in time it was shunned by the emerging orthodox world religions. Its temples desecrated, its philosophy maligned, its tradition spurned, its philosophy dormant in the mystical *Medu Neter*, the mysterious hieroglyphic texts which hold the secret symbolic meaning that has scarcely been discerned up to now. What are the secrets of *Nehast* {spiritual awakening and emancipation, resurrection}. More than just a literal translation, this volume is for awakening to the secret code *Shetitu* of the teaching which was not deciphered by Egyptologists, nor could be understood by ordinary spiritualists. This book is a reinstatement of the original science made available for our times, to the reincarnated followers of Ancient Egyptian culture and the prospect of spiritual freedom to break the bonds of *Khemn,* "ignorance," and slavery to evil forces: *Såaa* .

AND THE PHILOSOPHY OF RIGHTEOUS ACTION

30. EGYPTIAN MYSTERIES VOL 2: Dictionary of Gods and Goddesses ISBN: 1-884564-23-2 $21.95 This book is about the mystery of neteru, the gods and goddesses of Ancient Egypt (Kamit, Kemet). Neteru means "Gods and Goddesses." But the Neterian teaching of Neteru represents more than the usual limited modern day concept of "divinities" or "spirits." The Neteru of Kamit are also metaphors, cosmic principles and vehicles for the enlightening teachings of Shetaut Neter (Ancient Egyptian-African Religion). Actually they are the elements for one of the most advanced systems of spirituality ever conceived in human history. Understanding the concept of neteru provides a firm basis for spiritual evolution and the pathway for viable culture, peace on earth and a healthy human society. Why is it important to have gods and goddesses in our lives? In order for spiritual evolution to be possible, once a human being has accepted that there is existence after death and there is a transcendental being who exists beyond time and space knowledge, human beings need a connection to that which transcends the ordinary experience of human life in time and space and a means to understand the transcendental reality beyond the mundane reality.

31. EGYPTIAN MYSTERIES VOL. 3 The Priests and Priestesses of Ancient Egypt ISBN: 1-884564-53-4 $22.95 This volume details the path of Neterian priesthood, the joys, challenges and rewards of advanced Neterian life, the teachings that allowed the priests and priestesses to manage the most long lived civilization in human history and how that path can be adopted today; for those who want to tread the path of the Clergy of Shetaut Neter.

32. THE KING OF EGYPT: The Struggle of Good and Evil for Control of the World and The Human Soul ISBN 1-8840564-44-5 $18.95 This volume contains a novelized version of the Asarian Resurrection myth that is based on the actual scriptures presented in the Book Asarian Religion (old name –Resurrecting Osiris). This volume is prepared in the form of a screenplay and can be easily adapted to be used as a stage play. Spiritual seeking is a mythic journey that has many emotional highs and lows, ecstasies and depressions, victories and frustrations. This is the War of Life that is played out in the myth as the struggle of Heru and Set and those are mythic characters that represent the human Higher and Lower self. How to understand the war and emerge victorious in the journey o life? The ultimate victory and fulfillment can be experienced, which is not changeable or lost in time. The purpose of myth is to convey the wisdom of life through the story of divinities who show the way to overcome the challenges and foibles of life. In this volume the feelings and emotions of the characters of the myth have been highlighted to show the deeply rich texture of the Ancient Egyptian myth. This myth contains deep spiritual teachings and insights into the nature of self, of God and the mysteries of life and the means to discover the true meaning of life and thereby achieve the true purpose of life. To become victorious in the battle of life means to become the King (or Queen) of Egypt.Have you seen movies like The Lion King, Hamlet, The Odyssey, or The Little Buddha? These have been some of the most popular movies in modern times. The Sema Institute of Yoga is dedicated to researching and presenting the wisdom and culture of ancient Africa. The Script is designed to be produced as a motion picture but may be addapted for the theater as well. $19.95 copyright 1998 By Dr. Muata Ashby

33. FROM EGYPT TO GREECE: The Kamitan Origins of Greek Culture and Religion ISBN: 1-884564-47-X $22.95 U.S. FROM EGYPT TO GREECE This insightful manual is a quick reference to Ancient Egyptian mythology and philosophy and its correlation to what later became known as Greek and Rome mythology and philosophy. It outlines the basic tenets of the mythologies and shoes the ancient origins of Greek culture in Ancient Egypt. This volume also acts as a resource for Colleges students who would like to set up fraternities and sororities based on the original Ancient Egyptian principles of Sheti and Maat philosophy. ISBN: 1-884564-47-X $22.95 U.S.

34. THE FORTY TWO PRECEPTS OF MAAT, THE PHILOSOPHY OF RIGHTEOUS ACTION AND THE ANCIENT EGYPTIAN WISDOM TEXTS ADVANCED STUDIES This manual is designed for use with the 1998 Maat Philosophy Class conducted by Dr. Muata Ashby. This is a detailed study of Maat Philosophy. It contains a compilation of the 42 laws or precepts of Maat and the corresponding principles which they represent along with the teachings of the ancient Egyptian Sages relating to each. Maat philosophy was the basis of Ancient Egyptian society and government as well as the heart of Ancient Egyptian myth and spirituality. Maat is at once a goddess, a cosmic force and a living social doctrine, which promotes social harmony and thereby paves the way for spiritual evolution in all levels of society. ISBN: 1-884564-48-8 $16.95 U.S.

MUSIC BASED ON THE PRT M HRU AND OTHER KEMETIC TEXTS

Available on Compact Disc $14.99 and Audio Cassette $9.99

Adorations to the Goddess

Music for Worship of the Goddess

NEW Egyptian Yoga Music CD
by Sehu Maa
Ancient Egyptian Music CD
Instrumental Music played on reproductions of Ancient Egyptian Instruments– Ideal for meditation and reflection on the Divine and for the practice of spiritual programs and Yoga exercise sessions.

©1999 By Muata Ashby
CD $14.99 –

MERIT'S INSPIRATION
NEW Egyptian Yoga Music CD
by Sehu Maa
Ancient Egyptian Music CD
Instrumental Music played on reproductions of Ancient Egyptian Instruments– Ideal for meditation and reflection on the Divine and for the practice of spiritual programs and Yoga exercise sessions.
©1999 By
Muata Ashby
CD $14.99 –
UPC# 761527100429

ANORATIONS TO RA AND HETHERU
NEW Egyptian Yoga Music CD
By Sehu Maa (Muata Ashby)
Based on the Words of Power of Ra and HetHeru
played on reproductions of Ancient Egyptian Instruments **Ancient Egyptian Instruments used: Voice, Clapping, Nefer Lute, Tar Drum, Sistrums, Cymbals** – The Chants, Devotions, Rhythms and Festive Songs Of the Neteru – Ideal for meditation, and devotional singing and dancing.

©1999 By Muata Ashby
CD $14.99 –
UPC# 761527100221

SONGS TO ASAR ASET AND HERU
NEW
Egyptian Yoga Music CD
By Sehu Maa
played on reproductions of Ancient Egyptian Instruments– The Chants, Devotions, Rhythms and Festive Songs Of the Neteru - Ideal for meditation, and devotional singing and dancing.
Based on the Words of Power of Asar (Asar), Aset (Aset) and Heru (Heru) Om Asar Aset Heru is the third in a series of musical explorations of the Kemetic (Ancient Egyptian) tradition of music. Its ideas are based on the Ancient Egyptian Religion of Asar, Aset and Heru and it is designed for listening, meditation and worship. ©1999 By Muata Ashby
CD $14.99 –
UPC# 761527100122

HAARI OM: ANCIENT EGYPT MEETS INDIA IN MUSIC
NEW Music CD
By Sehu Maa

The Chants, Devotions, Rhythms and
Festive Songs Of the Ancient Egypt and India, harmonized and played on reproductions of ancient instruments along with modern instruments and beats. Ideal for meditation, and devotional singing and dancing.
Haari Om is the fourth in a series of musical explorations of the Kemetic (Ancient Egyptian) and Indian traditions of music, chanting and devotional spiritual practice. Its ideas are based on the Ancient Egyptian Yoga spirituality and Indian Yoga spirituality.

©1999 By Muata Ashby
CD $14.99 –
UPC# 761527100528

RA AKHU: THE GLORIOUS LIGHT
NEW
Egyptian Yoga Music CD
By Sehu Maa

The fifth collection of original music compositions based on the Teachings and Words of The Trinity, the God Asar and the Goddess Nebethet, the Divinity Aten, the God Heru, and the Special Meditation Hekau or Words of Power of Ra from the Ancient Egyptian Tomb of Seti I and more...
played on reproductions of Ancient Egyptian Instruments and modern instruments - **Ancient Egyptian Instruments used: Voice, Clapping, Nefer Lute, Tar Drum, Sistrums, Cymbals**
– The Chants, Devotions, Rhythms and Festive Songs Of the Neteru – Ideal for meditation, and devotional singing and dancing.

©1999 By Muata Ashby
CD $14.99 –
UPC# 761527100825

GLORIES OF THE DIVINE MOTHER
Based on the hieroglyphic text of the worship of Goddess Net.
The Glories of The Great Mother
©2000 Muata Ashby
CD $14.99 UPC# 761527101129`

Order Form

Telephone orders: Call Toll Free: 1(305) 378-6253. Have your AMEX, Optima, Visa or MasterCard ready.

Fax orders: 1-(305) 378-6253 E-MAIL ADDRESS: Semayoga@aol.com

Postal Orders: Sema Institute of Yoga, P.O. Box 570459, Miami, Fl. 33257. USA.

Please send the following books and / or tapes.

ITEM

________________________________Cost $________
________________________________Cost $________
________________________________Cost $________
________________________________Cost $________
________________________________Cost $________
Total $________

Name:____
Physical Address:______________________________________
City:________________ State:______ Zip:________

Sales tax: Please add 6.5% for books shipped to Florida addresses
________Shipping: $6.50 for first book and .50¢ for each additional
________Shipping: Outside US $5.00 for first book and $3.00 for each additional

_____Payment:______________________________
_____Check -Include Driver License #:
____

_____Credit card: _____ Visa, _____ MasterCard, _____ Optima, _____ AMEX.

Card number:________________________________
Name on card:___________________________ Exp. date:_____/______

Sema Institute of Yoga
P.O.Box 570459, Miami, Florida, 33257
(305) 378-6253 Fax: (305) 378-6253

Printed in Great Britain
by Amazon